# THE $100 MILLION EXIT

# THE
# $100 MILLION
# EXIT

## YOUR ROADMAP TO
## THE ULTIMATE PAYDAY

## JONATHAN BRABRAND

NEW DEGREE PRESS

THE $100 MILLION EXIT

*Your Roadmap to the Ultimate Payday*

ISBN     978-1-64137-517-7  *Paperback*

          978-1-64137-518-4  *Kindle Ebook*

          978-1-64137-519-1  *Ebook*

# CONTENTS

---

# AUTHOR'S NOTE

—

I have spent my entire professional career, over twenty years and counting, leading sell-side mergers and acquisitions (M&A) transactions as an investment banker. Simply put, I represent owners of businesses in the $10–200 million range and find buyers for their companies.

Over the dozens of transactions I've closed, I have seen example after example of best practices that my clients have employed to maximize their exit. But these lessons lie hidden away from public view, behind closed office doors, and on confidential calls.

Rather than let them go to waste, I reveal in this book the eleven most powerful lessons I've learned over my career in the hopes that readers will use them to their benefit.

To bring these lessons to life, I have included narratives in which I pull the curtain back on the highly confidential inner workings of real M&A transactions.

*The details of the M&A deals that you'll read about have never been made public before now.*

To share these insider stories with you, I have changed any identifying characteristics, including names, industries, lines of business, and geographies, to protect the privacy of the parties involved.

# INTRODUCTION

---

One law, virtually unknown outside of the world of mergers and acquisitions, has the power to kill billion-dollar deals. Commonly known as HSR, The Hart-Scott-Rodino Antitrust Improvements Act of 1976 is the federal government's antitrust Hellfire missile. This law requires that each and every US merger and acquisition transaction over $90 million must be reviewed by the Federal Trade Commission (FTC) or Department of Justice (DOJ) before the deal can close.[1] The DOJ or FTC assesses whether the deal would harm competition or consumers, and if so, these agencies can require changes to the deal, such as spinning off assets in a particular market to a third party, or they can block the transaction entirely. If the parties chose to move forward with the blocked deal anyway, in violation of HSR, they can be fined up to $42,530 per day.[2] The HSR review process can kill any deal, including the largest.

---

1    (Sidley 2019)

2    Ibid.

While most transactions that undergo HSR review are approved, a small portion, typically 2–4 percent, of deals are not. According to the FY 2018 Hart-Scott-Rodino Annual Report, of the 2,111 transactions reviewed that year, the FTC and DOJ challenged thirty-nine of them, or 2 percent of the total.[3]

The HSR process has killed deals involving the combinations of well-known companies such as food distributors US Foods and Sysco, and more recently DraftKings and FanDuel of fantasy sports fame, as well as those involving companies you've never heard of. In my twenty-year career as an investment banker representing middle-market companies for sale, I have even had the rare personal experience of having one of my deals struck down by the HSR review process. So, I know firsthand, better than most, what the HSR process entails.

But the event that surprised me the most, which set in motion my quest to uncover this and other exit lessons for business owners buried within large M&A successes and failures, was not a deal that died at the hands of HSR, but the explicit *approval* of a deal that created a clear consumer-facing monopoly: the 2008 combination of Sirius Satellite Radio and XM Satellite Radio. This triggered a few questions for me on the matter:

*How were the only two satellite radio companies in the US allowed to combine?*

---

3   (Simons and Delrahim 2018)

*Why was that deal approved when seemingly less-concerning mergers had been blocked?*

The answers to these questions provide valuable insight for business owners. Over the past year, I've been obsessed with analyzing why large exits, those valued at $100 million or more, succeed or fail to see what lessons may exist that would be applicable to M&A transactions of all sizes. As a business owner, wouldn't it be valuable to understand what these large companies did or didn't do well that led to their successful or failed M&A pursuits, and then apply that insider knowledge proactively in your exit?

Turns out, whether you want to exit in twelve months or twelve years, there is, indeed, much that we can learn from $100 million M&A successes and failures.

Middle market businesses, or those valued at less than $100 million, represent most of the M&A volume in North America. Industry data-source PitchBook notes that 70 percent of the 111,800 M&A transactions that occurred in the 2009–2018 timeframe were valued at less than $100 million.[4] In reality, while nearly every transaction above $100 million is reported, many smaller deals are not publicly announced or otherwise tracked, so the proportion of sub-$100 million deals is even higher. Yet most owners of middle-market businesses are leaving significant money on the table when compared to their peers that own companies valued over $100 million.

---

4    (PitchBook Data, Inc. 2019)

Based on research by GF Data® on 261 private transactions in 2018 that were priced less than $250 million, deals in the $10–25 million range traded for an average of 5.9x EBITDA (earnings before interest, taxes, depreciation, and amortization), while transactions valued in the $100–250 million range traded for an average of 8.8x EBITDA.[5] That difference equates to larger transactions' receiving a size premium of just under 50 percent. If you were selling a business with $2 million of EBITDA, that means an *extra* $5.8 million.

Business owners often subscribe to a set of mistaken assumptions about how companies in general, and their company in particular, are sold. They believe that when they are ready to sell, the best buyer, or perhaps even their own employees, will jump at the opportunity to acquire the business and make them a great offer. They believe that the process of completing the sale of their business will be relatively quick and painless, perhaps only a little more involved than a real estate transaction, and that they, along with their trusted local business attorney, can complete the deal without any additional outside help. Business owners also believe that the value of their business is driven by their company's historical performance and the value of its hard assets. Finally, they are pretty sure they know who the best buyer will be based on their industry contacts.

But I believe something else entirely.

I believe that the most successful M&A transactions don't just happen passively; they are achieved through hard work.

---

5    (GF Data Resources LLC 2019)

Getting top dollar for your business requires specific and proactive action that begins years before you are ready to exit, continues through the sale process, and doesn't end until months after the deal has closed. At times, it will feel like you've taken on a second full-time job. I believe the unequivocally best way to sell your company is through a professionally managed M&A process, which will take nine to twelve months from start to finish and will be worth every minute. I believe a company's value is equal parts objective and subjective and is highly dependent on the buyer's point of view on the company's future performance. It pays to remember that buyers are buying the company's *future*, not its *past*, though they will look to recent history to validate their views of the future. I believe the best buyer for your business will most likely be one you have never even heard of, not the one you are picturing.

I have spent over two decades leading sell-side M&A transactions as an investment banker, which simply means I represent owners in the sale of their companies. Like a realtor sells homes, I find buyers for $10–200 million companies. I love helping founders and other business owners achieve their personal and financial goals and begin new life chapters by exiting their business. Just as importantly, the companies themselves get a new lease on life with the next owner, ensuring they will continue operating long after the previous owner has retired.

Over the course of my career, I have seen numerous instances in which business owners left significant money on the table or had their deal with a great buyer completely fall apart because they took the "For Sale by Owner" approach and weren't prepared. It pains me, professionally and personally, to see what should be the exciting culmination of years, decades, or even generations of work, end in a disappointing outcome or an altogether failed deal. One story stands out.

Husband and wife business owners, Jim and Agnes Crawford, had built a profitable property management business over the past ten years. I was introduced to the Crawfords several years earlier through a family connection and had always admired the company they were building. Like many owners, they received periodic inquiries to sell from local competitors and out-of-state players alike, but they always brushed them off. *"We have no plans to sell anytime soon,"* Agnes would say, *"and we don't want to share any confidential information on our company."* So, they would either ignore the inquiries or politely decline.

As the years went by and the Crawfords got closer to retirement, though, the idea of selling the business and traveling the world in their golden years became more and more attractive. *"We loved the thought of securing our nest egg and having the free time to explore parts of the world we've only dreamed of visiting,"* Jim recalls. When one of the most aggressive consolidators in the property management industry approached them again, this time they took the meeting.

The Crawfords' initial meeting with the buyer went well by all accounts, and soon a tentative deal structure was being discussed. The Crawfords were smart business owners, but had never sold a business before, and so lacked any real experience in M&A transactions. Despite my offer to help, they moved forward with the buyer on their own and signed an agreement in principle, called a Letter of Intent (LOI), for an exit at what seemed to them to be an attractive valuation.

Soon, though, things started going downhill. In the months after signing the LOI, the Crawfords spent nights and weekends preparing responses to one information request list after another from the buyer. With no context on whether, how, or when to push back on the deluge of requests, Jim and Agnes were overwhelmed with the buyer's questions and let their attention slip from running the business. After nearly ninety days of due diligence, the buyer re-traded the deal by lowering the purchase price by more than 25 percent from the agreed-upon value, citing issues they uncovered in their diligence review. By this point, the Crawfords had had enough and walked away from the deal. When they woke up the next morning, Jim and Agnes had nothing to show for their work but hours of wasted time and a business that had plateaued due to lack of attention by its owners.

Not only was this episode a huge waste of time and effort for the Crawfords, but the overall prospect of selling their business suffered in two important ways. First, the once-positive relationship that the Crawfords enjoyed with that particular buyer was now damaged for the foreseeable future, so one of the best buyers for their business is no longer a viable option. Secondly, having a great buyer already at the table is a powerful way to begin a competitive M&A process that would have yielded a market-clearing price. But the chance to start their process from a position of strength was squandered.

With this book, I want to free business owners from costly, avoidable mistakes and deal pitfalls like those that the

Crawfords experienced. Knowing that larger deals sell for much higher multiples, I set out to discover the lessons that can be learned from both failed and successful $100 million exits that owners of any-sized businesses can apply to dramatically improve their chances of success in the sale of their own company.

This book is designed to speak directly to business owners, or to their trusted advisors, and provide them with practical, real-world advice that they can apply in their company today to be better prepared to maximize their exit. I don't want business owners to leave money on the closing table or worse yet, fail to complete their sale like the Crawfords. In this book, you'll discover the fundamental drivers behind the successes and failures of a representative sample of $100 million exits, including:

- A founder who grew his business from $25 million in revenue to over $750 million by selling the company three times to different private equity groups

- A business owner who tried twice to sell his company without an M&A advisor, failing both times, before engaging an investment bank that ran a well-executed M&A process and achieved a lucrative sale of the company

- The five partners of a high-growth IT consulting firm who were happy to skip over the top two bidders and choose the third-highest buyer to acquire their business, a decision that cost each of them more than $1 million

*The $100 Million Exit* contains eleven chapters grouped into three parts. While the chapters are presented in the chronological order that most sellers would experience them, each chapter stands alone and can be read out of sequence. I have included specific takeaways that you can put into practice in your business at the end of each chapter, and you can find the entire list of these action items summarized in the Conclusion.

- **Part 1: Achieving a Sale-Ready Posture,** contains Chapters 1–4, and covers how to plant seeds with potential industry buyers before you are ever ready to sell, how to manage your business like buyers will expect, how to create a business with intrinsic value apart from your personal involvement, and how to know when the time to exit has arrived.

- **Part 2: Kicking Off the M&A Process,** contains Chapters 5–8. Here, we learn why you need an M&A advisor and how to find the best one for your process, how to methodically prepare for the M&A process to retain negotiating leverage and momentum throughout, how to use positioning strategies to attract aggressive buyers, and how to fully understand the available exit options so you can pursue those that match your desired outcome.

- **Part 3: Winning the M&A Process,** contains Chapters 9–11 and focuses on the final phase of an M&A process. We will learn that there are more important factors to maximize other than solely price, that minimizing surprises is the key to avoiding a re-trade, and that you should keep the deal as simple as possible.

It is often said that those who do not understand history are doomed to repeat it. I hope this book provides you the lessons you need to replicate these real-world M&A successes and avoid these real-world M&A failures.

Are you ready for the roadmap that leads to your ultimate payday? *Let's go.*

# PART 1

# ACHIEVING A SALE-READY POSTURE

# CHAPTER 1

# DEVELOP INDUSTRY RELATIONSHIPS

---

The first lesson I learned from analyzing $100 million exits is that successful sellers often started laying the groundwork for their eventual sale many years before they planned to exit. They called it achieving a "sale-ready" posture. Someone once told me, *"everyone will exit their business sooner or later; the secret is being in a constant state of readiness so you can take advantage when an opportunity to exit presents itself."* If you aren't prepared, you may still get the deal closed, but not at the value you could have realized, or the deal may fall apart and you'll have missed the opportunity altogether.

> If you aren't prepared, you may still get the deal closed, but not at the value you could have realized, or the deal may fall apart and you'll have missed the opportunity altogether.

The beauty of adopting a sale-ready approach is that it has two powerful benefits. First, it will make the eventual exit of your business easier, faster, and more lucrative, whenever and however that exit event may come. Business owners in a sale-ready position have invested the time in laying the groundwork that will enable a thoughtful, smooth transition into a sale or other capital-raising process. It will also enable you to respond quickly if you unexpectedly receive an attractive unsolicited offer from a potential buyer.

Second, the process of preparing your business for sale will make your business better, *today*. Business owners with a sale-ready mind-set think more strategically, have better insights into their companies, and make better decisions on where to take their business next. They, therefore, create a two-fold benefit: when the time comes to exit, they have a more valuable business and are better prepared to exit. With this in mind, why wait?

* * *

Maintaining a sale-ready posture comes from actions that are both *internally* and *externally* focused. In this chapter, we'll look at external actions. In the next, we'll address internal preparations, which comprise setting the company's strategic direction and adopting improved and more formalized management techniques.

External activities involve raising the company's profile in the industry and building relationships with potential future business partners, buyers, and investors. In addition, the information gleaned from these external conversations will yield valuable insights that can then, in turn, influence your internal decision-making process in the near-term.

> External activities involve raising the company's profile in the industry and building relationships with potential future business partners, buyers, and investors. In addition, the information gleaned from these external conversations will yield valuable insights that can then, in turn, influence your internal decision-making process in the near-term.

## PLANTING SEEDS FOR THE FUTURE

One of the best examples of external sale readiness comes from Fletcher Graham, a successful entrepreneur who lives with his wife and three school-aged kids in Raleigh, North Carolina. When Fletcher decided to leave a lucrative investment banking career to launch Everest Motors, a new company with an innovative model for selling pre-owned vehicles, he not only wanted to disrupt the $118 billion used car industry,[6] he also wanted to use external sale-readiness tactics to raise start-up capital. Fletcher leveraged his extensive investment banking background to adopt these practices from the earliest days of his new company and continues to apply them today.

---

6    (IBISWorld 2019)

After beginning his professional career in public accounting, Fletcher transitioned to the fast-paced and challenging world of investment banking. He first worked on Wall Street at Lehman Brothers, where he was part of a team that helped clients, typically multibillion-dollar companies, raise equity capital. He saw how the executives from public companies spent time with equity research analysts to explain their past results and outline their plans for future growth. This practice stimulated interest in their company with equity research firms, and, in turn, the investing public who then wanted to buy shares, driving stock prices higher and increasing shareholder value.

After Wall Street, Fletcher went back to school, earning an MBA from Yale University, and joined a high-end middle-market investment banking firm specializing in M&A. There, he again saw the power of Chief Executive Officers (CEOs) communicating their strategic vision to potential buyers during the sale process. That created excitement that drove valuation levels higher. When he decided after several years to move from selling other people's companies to creating and building one of his own, Fletcher applied these lessons to fund his new business.

From the beginning, while he was still building the Everest Motors business plan, Fletcher began laying the groundwork to raise his initial round of start-up capital. He networked with potential angel investors in Raleigh and the surrounding region through a series of one-on-one meetings, months before he needed to start fundraising. Fletcher recalls, *"I thought that if I built a small network of interested investors, shared with them the near-term goals that I had set for myself, and then circled back with them after having accomplished those goals, I would build personal credibility and draw them into a connection with the business."*

Over a period of months, Fletcher shared multiple examples of goals that he had set for himself and then achieved. Only then did Fletcher begin to solicit start-up capital, successfully raising the $500,000 he needed to fund the first Everest Motors location. *"If I'd shown up to my initial investor meetings with my newly minted business plan and my hand out for $500,000, I'd have been laughed out of the room,"* Fletcher noted. By waiting to ask for the start-up capital until after he'd demonstrated early successes and gained credibility, the investors were excited to get on board.

> By waiting to ask for the start-up capital until after he'd demonstrated early successes and gained credibility, the investors were excited to get on board.

After opening the first Everest Motors location and demonstrating the viability of his disruptive business model, Fletcher started thinking about the company's next phase of growth. He knew that at some point soon, he would need new investors with deeper pockets to fund the company's growth into a multisite, regional operation. *"I took the same approach that served me well with my angel investors but applied it to a new set of bigger investors: private equity groups."* He reasoned that this external sale-readiness tactic would work just as well with PE firms, which are similar to angel investors, but target companies that are more established.

Fletcher researched PE firms that had successfully invested in the automotive retail industry and identified five or six that he thought would be ideal partners for the next phase of Everest's growth. *"I looked for connections to these PE firms within my professional network and asked for introductions, or just cold-called them if a connection wasn't available. Just as I had done before, I started a dialogue with them months before we were ready to raise the growth capital we needed to expand,"* Fletcher recounts. He used the same external sale-readiness plan as he had with the angel investors, sharing progress milestones and updates on his business, all before broaching the topic of raising a new round of investment.

When Fletcher was ready to put his expansion plans into action, he raised $20 million of growth capital at an implied valuation of more than $100 million from one of the private equity firms he had been courting. Over time, this firm had come to understand and appreciate Fletcher's long-term vision for Everest Motors and, just as importantly, believed that he could achieve it based on the trust that had been built along the way. *"The funniest part of that transaction,"* Fletcher notes, *"is that my new partner told me after making the investment that if they had first learned about the capital raise prior to getting to know me and my vision for Everest Motors, they would have passed on the deal without a second thought."* By Fletcher's investing in the relationship with the PE firm well before needing their capital, Everest Motors secured a strong partner to support its growth that would otherwise have been uninterested.

In the years since he founded Everest Motors, the company has grown to twelve locations in five states, and Fletcher continues to implement his strategy of sowing seeds with potential future partners. Now he meets with senior executives from large players in the automotive industry who might one day want to acquire Everest Motors a couple of times a year, typically in a casual setting like a coffee shop or airport lounge. *"I'm not ready to sell anytime soon, and we never discuss a potential exit. We just trade war stories of doing business in the world of used cars, talking about where we've been and where we're going. I'm planting seeds that I'll harvest sometime in the future."* It takes effort to maintain the schedule of these periodic conversations, but Fletcher knows it is well worth it.

While the next transaction is likely years away, Fletcher sees a two-fold value in building these relationships with future potential buyers. First, these buyers are noticing Everest Motors and are witnessing its successful expansion over an extended period. When the time comes for Fletcher and his PE partner to consider exiting, he and his company will be well-known entities with long track records of success. Secondly, the nuggets of intel Fletcher gleans from these informal, off-the-record conversations with industry executives provide more immediate value.

Fletcher recalls a recent coffee he shared in Denver with the Chief Financial Officer (CFO) of a large, publicly traded competitor. When Fletcher asked how the last business that they acquired was faring in their first year of ownership, the CFO remarked that it wasn't growing as fast as they'd planned. *"In fact,"* he said, *"the Board recently determined that the acquisition was not substantial enough, wasn't moving the needle enough, to warrant the cost and time we invested in acquiring and integrating the operation. We won't make that mistake again."* As the conversation moved on, Fletcher made a mental note of this offhand remark.

On the plane back to Raleigh that night, Fletcher reflected on the CFO's comment about his Board's disappointment in their last acquisition. Fletcher had learned something important about that company's acquisition strategy that could be useful to him going forward. When looking at future M&A targets, that buyer would prioritize size and scale over profitability, requiring future targets to be sizable enough to justify the time and expense involved in acquiring and integrating them.

> When looking at future M&A targets, that buyer would prioritize size and scale over profitability, requiring future targets to be sizable enough to justify the time and expense involved in acquiring and integrating them.

Fletcher made a note to discuss this insight with his PE investors at their next Board meeting. If they wanted to someday attract this buyer's attention, they might need to consider moving up the timeline on Everest's national expansion plans.

\* \* \*

Savvy business owners look down the strategic path their company is on and seek opportunities to plant seeds for the future with potential partners, investors, and buyers. Investing the time to build relationships and establish credibility within your sector well ahead of any particular request will yield dividends today, in the form of useful market intelligence that can influence your strategic direction, and down the line, when you're ready to begin your company's next chapter.

**ACTION ITEMS**

- *Plant seeds for the future.* Think strategically about which types of partners, investors, or buyers will take your company to the next level. Conduct research to pick specific targets and use LinkedIn, industry trade shows, or cold calling to establish contact. Schedule informal meetings, ideally in person, with each group to share insights and your near-term goals, following up on the status of those on the next visit.

- *Incorporate market intel into your growth strategy.* Make note of the key takeaways and insights from your industry conversations and incorporate relevant pieces into your strategic plan. How valuable would it be to know what a potential buyer in your industry is looking for while there's still time to shape your company in that mold? While you may not implement every bit of intel you receive, make note of them all, use what makes sense for where you want to take your company, and file the rest away to revisit twelve to twenty-four months later.

# CHAPTER 2

# RUN YOUR BUSINESS LIKE A PRO

---

The phrase *"business owners would be wise to spend more time working on their business than in their business"* goes to the heart of achieving and maintaining an internal sale-ready state. The goal is to develop, implement, and maintain a variety of professional management techniques that will help you lead your business more effectively, and in so doing, also keep it in a sale-ready posture.

> The goal is to develop, implement, and maintain a variety of professional management techniques that will help you lead your business more effectively, and in so doing, also keep it in a sale-ready posture.

\* \* \*

Miguel Santos is a believer in the power of maintaining a sale-ready state through adherence to professional management techniques. As CEO of ACE Consolidated, a $250 million third-party logistics (3PL) provider sold four times during his tenure, he saw how a rigorous adherence to a strategic operating plan helped his company secure the funding it needed to avoid bankruptcy after the Great Recession of 2008. In another capacity as a board member of a private-equity backed company, Miguel saw how the *lack* of a strategic plan *reduced* the value of this high-growth company by more than 15 percent, turning what would have been an excellent investment into only a mediocre one. As a potential investor alongside another PE firm, Miguel saw how the absence of a coherent growth plan cast doubt on the ability of that company's CEO to scale the business beyond its current footprint, ultimately causing Miguel's partners to pass on the deal. In these and many more instances over the course of his decades-long professional career, Miguel has witnessed first-hand just how much of an impact a strategic plan can make.

Miguel didn't always want to be a CEO; he began his professional career as an attorney. After graduating from the University of Richmond, Miguel received his JD from the prestigious University of Pennsylvania Law School and spent the next seven years in private practice.

Working in the corporate law section, Miguel enjoyed helping his clients with the legal side of their operations, including acquisitions, divestitures, and restructurings, but wanted more. "*As much as I liked the law, I was more interested in how my clients developed and executed strategy,*" Miguel recalls. This curiosity led him back to school, earning an MBA from the University of Virginia's Darden School of Business. It was at Darden that Miguel first learned about the professional management techniques that would serve him well over the course of his career.

Upon graduation, Miguel joined ACE Consolidated, a small but growing publicly traded 3PL based in Boston as General Counsel and VP of Corporate Development, drawing on both his legal and business backgrounds. Miguel loved the operational challenges of growing a business in the logistics industry and remained at ACE for the next twenty years in successively senior roles, ultimately spending eleven years as its President and CEO. During his tenure at the company, ACE expanded through twenty acquisitions across the US and into the UK, Europe, and Asia, more than doubling earnings and driving revenue to $250 million annually.

ACE Consolidated went through four exits during Miguel's tenure with the company, two of which while he was CEO. The first was a take-private transaction backed by financial investors, then a sale several years later to a large strategic buyer. When the Great Recession hit and the logistics industry slumped, the strategic owner focused on core operations and spun ACE off to a hedge fund that used an excessive amount of debt to acquire the business. ACE suffered under the new debt load, despite performing well operationally, and was on the brink of bankruptcy when an operationally oriented private equity buyer stepped in as ACE's fourth owner, investing fresh capital to reduce the debt load and support the company's continued growth.

While strategic planning had always been central to ACE's culture, it was most valuable during the company's fourth transaction, the one that averted bankruptcy. *"If we hadn't developed a strong strategic plan, potential investors would not have been able to see that ACE had a debt-load problem, not an operational problem,"* Miguel explains. In fact, he credits his company's adherence to its strategic operating plan as the deciding factor in getting that transaction done and avoiding disaster.

Miguel's leadership philosophy is simple and just as applicable whether you lead a public or private company. *"As leader, your job, first and foremost, is to ensure that you have a sound strategy that makes sense in the marketplace, acknowledges the various restraints that are placed upon your company, and puts the company's resources to their highest and best use."* But *creating* a well-designed plan is just the first part.

> Sale-Ready Pro Tip: The business leader's job is to ensure the company's strategic plan: (1) makes sense in the market; (2) acknowledges the various restraints that exist; (3) puts the company's resources to their highest and best use.

The second part, once you have developed that plan, is to execute against it. In Miguel's view, *"Execution only comes with full strategic alignment, meaning that everybody in your organization understands and talks about the company's vision, its long-term plan and annual goals, and how those translate into their particular job position.*" In other words, a strategic plan is only as good as the employees' ability to understand and individually deliver their contribution to the overall mission of the organization.

## HOW A STRATEGIC PLANNING GAMBLE SAVED THE COMPANY

In the aftermath of the Great Recession, ACE's future was in doubt. The company was drowning under an immense debt load, and Miguel was actively seeking a buyer to bring in the new capital desperately needed to help the business regain its footing. Yet buyers were hesitant to invest in the company, uncertain about whether it would ultimately survive or fail. Miguel's mission was to convince them that ACE's operational and growth strategies were sound, and that if not for the anchor of debt dragging it down, ACE would be healthy and growing. With the pressure building and the initial attempts to raise the capital failing, Miguel made an unconventional and risky move.

He bet the company's future on how well his employees adhered to ACE's strategic plan.

Miguel proposed that the top potential investor talk not just to his direct reports, which is standard, but also to those employees that were two and three levels below him in the organization, as well as to its front-line staff. Without Miguel present, the buyer could see for themselves if everyone understood and was on board with ACE's strategic vision and beyond that, knew their role in achieving it.

As Miguel put it, "*As a leader, you have to have the confidence to let someone else talk to your people and take the temperature as to whether everybody's really rowing in the same direction.*" The investor held a dozen or so one-on-one interviews with employees from all levels of the company and was impressed with the results. Employees really did understand the strategy and could articulate how their role furthered it. Miguel's gamble paid off, as the interviews gave the financial buyer the confidence it needed in ACE's core business to make the much-needed investment to ensure the company's future.

### THE LACK OF STRATEGIC PLANNING CAN REALLY HURT

Miguel also witnessed firsthand how the lack of strategic planning can negatively impact an M&A exit.

In one such case, Miguel served on the board of a PE-backed company in a related industry to help provide market insights and general corporate oversight. The business had grown nicely under the leadership of an opportunistic CEO, but suffered from a lack of clear strategic direction and certainly did not have a formal strategic plan. When the time came for the private equity firm to exit, the investment bankers hired to sell the company created an impressive section in the offering memorandum on growth strategy, detailing the five ways in which the company would expand over the next several years.

What buyers would soon learn, however, was that these five growth strategies were not being pursued by management, a classic mistake of overly enthusiastic M&A advisors.

Based only on their review of the offering memorandum, potential buyers bid aggressively for the business, but when the top bidders were invited to meet management, the executive team didn't live up to the hype. Miguel recalls, *"In the management presentation, we had unrealistic financial projections, these hockey stick curves, based on entering market segments that we'd never been in, nor could the CEO show any fundamental way that he had actually capitalized on such opportunities in the past."* With no demonstrable proof of executing against a strategic plan to point to, the CEO came off looking more lucky than good. As a result, buyers either dropped out of the process entirely or lowered their valuations significantly. Ultimately, the company did sell, but at a price more than 15 percent lower than where valuations had been prior to management presentations. In this case, it was easy to quantify the cost of not having a strategic plan.

In another instance, Miguel was on the buyer's side of the table, partnering with a private equity firm to investigate potentially acquiring an attractive business in the medical transportation space. The company's business model focused on securely transporting blood and other medical samples from hospitals to centralized testing facilities. The company had grown to more than $30 million in revenue, largely driven by trends in the industry toward centralized testing facilities fueled by consolidation within the healthcare system. The company's geographic footprint had expanded quickly and included six cities, with plans for further expansion into additional markets.

As Miguel and his PE partner dug in deeper, however, red flags started to emerge. They learned that the company's six cities operated completely autonomously, with no unifying strategic plan, and they were having trouble replicating the successful aspects of the operation from one city to the other. *"Every city was sort of succeeding or struggling based on its own operational plan,"* Miguel realized. Furthermore, Miguel learned that each location was primarily driven by one anchor client, creating a customer concentration risk for each regional division.

In the end, Miguel and his PE partner decided the company wasn't worth backing and dropped out of the process. Miguel recalls, *"We had to ask ourselves if there was something that was replicable here, if there was a platform that we can build on."* Based on the lack of an operational plan, the answer was decidedly no.

Buyers seek to acquire companies at an inflection point, where their capital and partnership can make an exponential difference to the future of the business. Your ability to show potential buyers how you created strategic plans and executed upon them in the past will give them the confidence to believe in your current strategic plan and in how they and their capital can help support it going forward. In addition to being a great tool to manage your business outside of an exit process, developing a strategic, actionable, and relevant plan is a key step in maintaining a sale-ready posture. Let's look more closely at how you can implement this strategy in your business today.

At its core, internal sale readiness comprises three fundamental management techniques practiced in every company that achieves an exit of $100 million or more.

1. Set a strategic plan
2. Track data to monitor performance against plan
3. Report results to an accountability partner

(Repeat on an annual basis)

While the depth and frequency of each of these steps will vary based on the size of your company, you cannot afford to put this process off until some future date when your company is "big enough" to support it. Every business can implement these steps at an appropriate level of granularity. What's more important is that business owners set goals, use data to measure progress, and report on the outcome. Then the process repeats, using the information gathered from the previous cycle to create a revised, updated plan going forward.

## SET A STRATEGIC PLAN

Whether you engage a third-party facilitator to lead an off-site annual strategic planning session with your executive management team or create a simple growth plan in the quiet of your office, take the time on a quarterly, or at least annual, basis to step back, look up, and envision where you want your business to be headed.

As the famous Lewis Carroll quote reminds us, *"If you don't know where you are going, any road will get you there."* Building a business is too important to be left to chance. You will be much more successful by setting strategic goals so you know you are headed in the right direction.

What we are talking about here is not a business plan; this is a living strategy document with specific growth objectives that build into a detailed five-year financial forecast. It considers industry trends and market dynamics, as well as opportunities and threats you see on the horizon. It incorporates a candid, reality-based evaluation of your company's value proposition (why customers buy from you) and where your competitive advantages and disadvantages lie. It documents where you want the business to be in five years and what gaps you need to fill in to get there.

If you don't already have a strategic plan of this nature, I encourage you to start with a basic version and a modest level of detail at first. Rather than spend too much time creating one, or worse yet, avoiding even starting from a fear of how much effort it will require, I would rather you get a simple version in place and start benefiting from the strategic clarity it will provide. You can make the subsequent version of the plan more detailed and sophisticated next year.

### TRACK DATA TO MONITOR PROGRESS

Having access to accurate and timely data on the performance of your business enables you to track your progress against your strategic plan and make better leadership decisions based on data, not anecdotes or intuition. The challenge here is two-fold: determining what information to track and keeping the reporting process from becoming an inefficient time-sink.

Effective management reports begin with a GAAP-compliant, accrual (not cash-basis) three-statement set of financials (income statement, balance sheet, and statement of cash flows) that are closed on a monthly basis, and having the company's annual financials reviewed (or better yet, audited) by a well-known regional CPA firm. Executives of $100 million businesses also have one or more sets of dashboard reports that they review on a daily or weekly basis. These track the key financial and operational metrics that are most critical to your business and provide a more current view of the company's performance than monthly financials will allow, equipping management to react more quickly as needed.

## REPORT RESULTS TO AN ACCOUNTABILITY PARTNER

The value of setting a strategic plan and tracking data to monitor performance against that plan dramatically improves with the implementation of the third tool, a formal reporting process. The discipline of having to prepare and deliver a monthly, quarterly, and annual evaluation on how your company's actual results compared to plan is where the real strategic value is created. Instilling the habit of presenting analyses and updates on key strategic initiatives to a formal audience is powerful.

All companies over $100 million have an independent Board of Directors, most often comprising representatives from the owners, top executives, and outside industry professionals who are not otherwise affiliated with the company. Many of the more sophisticated companies under $100 million will have either a Board of Directors or less formal advisory board to provide accountability to the executives.

Even if your audience is your spouse or a trusted friend, it is critically important to establish the habit of preparing a Board package and delivering it to a third-party accountability partner. Set regular meeting dates with your Board and work diligently to keep them. Present both the areas of the business that exceeded the plan, but also those areas that fell short. Reporting the performance of your business, including being prepared to discuss the underlying reasons behind the results, will bring you more in tune with your company from a strategic perspective.

## RINSE AND REPEAT

As you approach the one-year anniversary of your current strategic plan, begin creating the next year's version by reviewing the new information gained over the past twelve months. Here you'll see your data-tracking efforts pay off, as you will have quantifiable metrics about where the business outperformed the plan and where it fell short. Roll the financial forecast model forward a year, modifying it as necessary based on the most recent actual results and adding a new fifth year to the projections.

> Sale-Ready Pro Tip: manage your business as if you already have a formal Board of Directors or an outside ownership group that will hold you accountable for delivering performance against your annual plan.

Implementing the simple three-step process outlined above will help you achieve a sale-ready posture, while at the same time, making you a better leader and helping your business grow faster. It will also show your future potential investors and buyers an impressive level of professionalism in how you run your business. Your next partner will already be executing these steps in their own company and will expect you to do the same soon after closing.

It will be all the easier if you're already in the habit.

* * *

Business owners who have successfully achieved $100 million exits started the preparation process many years before they planned to sell. They implemented internal management practices that provided clear direction for the future and detailed insights into the company's periodic performance versus plan. As we covered in the previous chapter, they also networked with potential future investors and buyers in their industry, building trust that might someday be important in a sale process, while also gaining strategic insights that can inform how the business operates today. In the next chapter, we will learn the importance of weaning yourself out of the daily activities of the business to create a company not dependent on your involvement, and thus more valuable.

## ACTION ITEMS

- *Take a new approach to your role.* As the leader of your business, one of your primary responsibilities is to make sure that your company has a strategic plan that includes the following three critical aspects.

- First, the plan must incorporate the market landscape and your company's competitive strengths and weaknesses relative to other industry participants. A traditional SWOT (strengths, weaknesses, opportunities, and threats) analysis can help here.

- Second, your plan should acknowledge the various real-world constraints that exist, including those related to financial capital and human capital, and work within them. Also, consider the related costs and benefits of removing one or more of these constraints.

- Third, the plan should ensure the company's resources are being put to their highest and best use. This includes everything from whether your products or services are targeting the most valuable end users, to whether your higher-paid employees could better leverage their time with the addition of lower-paid support resources.

- *Refine, implement, and revisit your plan.* Once you have developed your strategic plan, track specific data to measure your performance against plan, and then report your results to an outside accountability partner. Manage your business as if you already have a formal Board of Directors or an outside ownership group that will hold you accountable for delivering performance against your annual plan. Revisit your plan on a quarterly or annual basis and archive historical plans for future reference.

## CHAPTER 3

# BUILD A BUSINESS, NOT A JOB

---

The realization hit Jane like a punch in the gut. *"I haven't built a business at all. Bayside Financial is only a very profitable job. If I can't separate myself from my company, it will have no value when I want to retire."*

Businesses are more valuable than jobs.

Building a business is harder and much more complex than creating a job. Businesses create and amass long-term value, in addition to providing ongoing compensation, while jobs are only worth your current paycheck.

In other words, jobs provide income, but only while you're working at them, while businesses continue in perpetuity. Since businesses can be separated from their owners and continue operating, businesses can be sold but jobs cannot.

*How do you know if you have a business or a job?*

By asking yourself one simple question: *"Would my business be able to exist without me?"* If the answer is no, you have a job.

There's nothing wrong, per se, with owning your job. Many self-employed people have made a great living and built a fulfilling career by owning their job. A definite freedom comes from being one's own boss. If that is you, that may be all you care to do. But if you want to create something that has long-term value, something that can ultimately be monetized through a sale, you need to own a business or to transition your job *into* a business. And the key to that lies in your management team.

One of the most important factors that I've seen in over twenty years of M&A that drives a successful exit is the depth and quality of the management team. While this certainly includes the owners if they are actively involved in the business, what matters most is the team that reports to them. And more than just how good they are, the real question is:

*If the owners stopped showing up for work, who could keep the business moving forward?*

To you, as the owner, that person who could step up and move the business forward in your absence is your back-up, your bench, your understudy. They are your future successor, which is a critically important role that exists in virtually all $100 million companies, but one sorely lacking in most smaller businesses.

In fact, large companies will have designated successors for not only their owners, but for all the key leadership positions within the business. Whether that person is ready to step into your shoes tomorrow or three years from now is less important than whether that person exists within your organization and is on a development path, assuming more and more responsibilities within your company.

Having a strong management team that includes the owners' successor is critically important to a successful business in three important ways.

- First, it provides an insurance policy for the company's ability to survive upon the owner's retirement or should something unexpected happen to the owner in the meantime.

- Second, it dramatically expands the universe of potential buyers who will be interested in your business when it's time to exit.

- Third, it enables a smooth and successful transition to the next owner, significantly increasing the likelihood that you'll fully earn any purchase price contingent on your business's performance after closing.

Let's take a closer look at each of these three perspectives.


**INSURANCE POLICY**
Having a successor in your business serves as an insurance policy against unforeseen events. Jane Marbury owns a small,

five-person wealth management firm called Bayside Financial. Jane founded the business over fifteen years ago after leaving a similar practice within a national bank and hanging out her own shingle. Like many start-ups, Bayside was built around Jane's personal expertise, contacts, and business acumen. The clients that engage Bayside Financial to manage their assets do so in large part because of Jane.

One day, about five years ago during a family vacation, Jane was reflecting on Bayside and realized her firm was wholly dependent on her personal abilities. *"I had just turned sixty,"* Jane recalls, *"and I came to a startling realization: Bayside the firm and me the owner were one and the same. Bayside wouldn't exist without me."*

Following that train of thought, Jane reached the inevitable conclusion that whenever she retired, which was more and more in the back of her mind, Bayside would cease to exist. Bayside was Jane's job, not her business.

After that vacation, Jane set about finding a future successor for her business. Not a peer of hers that could take over on Day 1, but a protégée who could be groomed into the role over time. It took her a few months of searching, but Jane found her number two. Steve Bryant, a successful professional in his mid-thirties with significant experience in the wealth management industry, was looking for a more entrepreneurial opportunity. Jane brought Steve on board at Bayside and began developing his skills across all aspects of the firm.

After an initial trial period of eighteen months, Jane was confident that Steve was indeed a great candidate to be her successor and approached him about a formal long-term transition plan. *"The goal was to make it easy to understand and crystal clear,"* Jane notes. The agreement they reached was simple, yet effective. When Jane reached sixty-five years old, or otherwise retired from Bayside, the business would be valued using a predetermined formula. Steve would then take full ownership of the business and pay Jane the purchase price over a seven-year period funded by the earnings of the business.

By bringing Steve on board and creating a long-term transition plan, Jane successfully transitioned Bayside from a job to a business. Bayside now had value as an ongoing entity, and Jane knew that if something unexpected happened to her tomorrow, her clients and employees would be cared for, as would her family through the pay-out provision.

Having a succession plan in place also gave Jane significant leverage when she was later approached by a bank that wanted to acquire Bayside as part of an expansion of its financial services. Jane responded, *"I would be happy to entertain your proposal, but I am perfectly happy to exit Bayside through the arrangement I already have in place with Steve."* That arrangement with Steve gave Jane optionality and enabled her to negotiate from a position of strength. When she received the potential buyer's offer, which was less attractive than her buy-out plan with Steve, Jane was able to decline the offer without consternation or remorse and move forward undeterred.

The ability to have a successor in place to serve as an insurance policy against retirement or unexpected life events is just as effective in larger businesses as it is in a small firm like Bayside. Larger companies may have a pool of potential successor candidates to draw from internally, supplementing an external candidate search, but the need for a successor is equally as important. Whether it has two employees or fifty employees, a business with no one to step into the top owner's role is just a job.

## EXPANDED UNIVERSE OF POTENTIAL BUYERS

Companies with strong management teams and an identified successor for the owners will be attractive to a much broader universe of potential buyers when it comes time to exit. Said differently, businesses that lack a bench of talent are blocked out of consideration by an estimated 75 percent or more of the potential buyer universe. *The reason?* The only contenders interested in buying a business without a strong leadership team are local competitors or strategic buyers who can consolidate your operations into theirs. These buyers may see some value in your business, but it won't be as high as if other buyers were competing. Virtually all private equity groups, family offices, and other financial investors, as well as many corporate buyers, require an ongoing management team to back in companies they acquire. For the few financial investors that don't, their valuations will be lower to reflect the increased risk required to find a successor and successfully transition the business away from the owner after closing.

When I meet with business owners interested in selling, we spend a lot of time discussing how long they would like to remain active in their business, and in what specific roles. But we also delve into understanding the strength of their management team. Without a strong team to remain with the business on an ongoing basis after a transaction is completed, we know that our universe of potential buyers is limited, and with it, so too are the chances for a highly competitive M&A process that will yield a maximum value.

A former client of mine, Salisbury Electrical, is a perfect illustration. Salisbury was a highly profitable niche distribution business that carried a deep inventory of pre-owned electronic switchgear and other components that are no longer manufactured, providing valuable, hard-to-find replacement parts to support a large installed base of these products still in operation around the world. Rosemont had grown to over $15 million in revenue since its founding twelve years ago and was owned by three partners who served as the company's CEO, CFO, and COO. With the CEO and CFO nearing retirement age, the owners engaged me to run an M&A process to find a buyer for Salisbury.

During my initial due diligence, we learned that all three of the owners wanted to retire from the business over a six- to twelve-month period post-closing, and that none of the three had a successor in the company. In fact, the next most senior person within Salisbury was a counter salesperson with no managerial responsibilities or experience.

Despite a long list of attractive attributes, called investment merits, that would appeal to both financial and strategic buyers, the lack of management depth beyond the owners required us to eliminate the bulk of these prospective buyers. With no leadership team in place for a new buyer to back, we could only contact strategic buyers whose operations were close enough from a geographic and strategic perspective that they could fold Salisbury into their existing business model and reporting structure.

While we were ultimately able to find such a buyer, competition for the company was sparse. The value we received for the business, while acceptable to the owners, was far less than it could have been. If only Salisbury's shareholders had invested in a team of successors, we would have been able to run a much broader process with headier competition that would have yielded a much higher valuation.

### SUCCESSFUL TRANSITION

As a third benefit, companies with strong management teams that will remain in place post-closing are more likely to have a successful transition to the new buyer, which is important for at least two reasons.

First, most if not all business owners have a tremendous and well-earned amount of personal pride tied to the businesses they've built and want them to continue performing well after the sale as part of their legacy. I often find that this can be just as important as the economics of a transaction for my clients. In fact, I have seen founders pass over the highest bidder for their company to select the buyer they think will be best for the future of their company and their employees, costing them real money in the form of a lower purchase price. We'll see a concrete example of this in Chapter 9.

Successful transitions are also critical when a portion of the purchase price is dependent on the company's future performance after closing. These arrangements, called earn-outs, represent a portion of the purchase price, typically ranging 10–30 percent of the total, that will only be paid by the buyer if the company meets agreed-upon performance goals during a specific time period after closing, usually six to twenty-four months. Having a team in place that you trust running your business after it is sold can mean the difference between collecting or losing out on millions in incremental purchase price.

During his thirteen years with metal stamping company Advanced Engineering, the last three of which in the CFO role, Colin Baker led the acquisitions of ten privately held companies, ranging in price from below $10 million to well over $100 million. Advanced was experiencing a period of rapid growth, primarily by making acquisitions across the US and into Canada, as the company pursued a consolidation strategy within the highly fragmented metal stamping industry.

*"As I think about how the owners of the businesses we acquired would have rated their exits, I believe only one of the ten sellers would say his sale to Advanced Engineering was a success,"* Colin recalls. All ten transactions included an earn-out as a portion of the purchase price, and in nine of the deals, the former owners either prematurely left their businesses voluntarily, or were asked to leave, within twelve to eighteen months of selling and without fully achieving their earn-outs.

The owners of New Castle, an Ontario-based metal stamping company, however, continued to lead their company after selling to Advanced for several years before entering a planned hand-over period to their successors that facilitated their retirement. During that period, New Castle's founders met the earn-out targets to receive the full purchase price and ensured that the company was on solid footing for the benefit of its employees and other stakeholders going forward.

New Castle's two owners recognized early on the importance of having a long-term game plan for the leadership of their business, and so they identified and cultivated a layer of middle managers that could mature into key leadership positions in the company over time.

Colin summarizes their approach well. *"I think they were both really smart guys who were able to put their ego aside and realize that, with the right team in place, the business could run just as well without them. And if it did, then that would say more about them [as founders] than if the business didn't run well without them."* Rather than fall victim to the pride that many business owners feel in how critical they are to the success of their businesses, the owners of New Castle believed just the opposite: *the less dependent New Castle was on its owners, the better.*

New Castle's owners shared their succession plans with Advanced in their initial meetings and, later during due diligence, allowed Colin and his team to get to know the next generation of leaders. *"As the acquirer, we were able to get comfortable that New Castle had a well-crafted development plan for these managers, which dramatically reduced the risk that we always need to evaluate around former business owners' leaving or drastically scaling back once the purchase price hits their banking account,"* said Colin.

After closing, New Castle's owners continued to run the business, now a stand-alone division of Advanced, for three years, as agreed to as part of the transaction. This period allowed the business to settle into being part of a larger company, while still being overseen by its former owners and enabled the next generation of leaders to finish growing into their new responsibilities. It also allowed the former owners to continue operating the business during the earn-out evaluation period post-closing.

When the managers were promoted as planned into executive roles on the third anniversary of the transaction, New Castle's former owners first moved into part-time roles focused on special strategic projects. Six months later, they stepped further back into consulting roles on an as-needed basis. Then, a total of four years after selling their business, the owners fully retired, content in knowing their business would continue on well-run by their successors and well-supported by Advanced Engineering.

It is important to note that while the succession plan certainly benefited both the owners of New Castle and Advanced Engineering, improving the marketability of New Castle was not the plan's original goal. The owners simply wanted to know that their company would successfully outlast their personal involvement, that a contingency plan was in place should something unforeseen happen to either or both. It started out as an insurance policy and morphed into supporting a successful transition to the business's next owner.

\* \* \*

One of the most important drivers of a successful exit is having a strong second-level management team that will continue to lead the business after the exit. An internal succession plan serves as a valuable insurance policy against unforeseen events and significantly expands the universe of potential buyers that will be available when the time comes to exit. It also ensures a smooth transition to the next owner and maximizes any earn-out portion of the purchase price. An internal succession plan means the difference between building a business with intrinsic value and simply owning your own job.

> An internal succession plan means the difference between building a business with intrinsic value and simply owning your own job.

All business owners should remember that they will all exit their businesses at some point, one way or another. The question is whether or not it will be on their terms. In the next chapter, we will learn how to evaluate market conditions and know when the optimal time has arrived to exit your business.

## ACTION ITEMS

- **Build your bench.** Look around your organization and identify key individuals that could grow into long-term leaders for your business. Each of your top positions, including your role as President or CEO, should have an identified understudy. If holes exist, make it a priority to fill these positions. Invest in providing training and professional development for those individuals. Consider creating a long-term incentive program to retain them and allow them to participate in the value creation of the business over time. Talk with your attorney and accountants about programs such as options, phantom stock, and profit interests to accomplish this objective.

- *Slowly back away.* Start delegating responsibilities as soon as possible. If need be, begin slowly with small tasks or for short periods of time, such as while you're away on vacation. Provide mentoring, clear feedback, and support, with the goal of developing managers who can step into your shoes at some point in the future. Remember, having your succession plan in place, even though it isn't yet complete, is significantly better than not having started one at all.

# CHAPTER 4

# KNOW WHEN THE TIME IS RIGHT

———

Cerulli Associates projects that nearly forty-five million US households will transfer a total of $68.4 trillion in wealth to heirs and charity over the course of the next twenty-five years.[7]

For most owners, the goal of retiring from their business and realizing the wealth that has been created within their company drives their decision to sell. Others use a sale process to shift ownership to the next generation of family or to their employees to ensure the business will outlive its founder. For still others, an M&A transaction is a means of establishing a new and exciting chapter for the owner, the business, and the employees.

For serial entrepreneur, speaker, bestselling author, and business consultant Andy Stefanovich, selling his first business

———

7    (Cerulli Associates n.d.)

was all about new chapters. In 1990, at the age of twenty-four, Andy founded Opus Event Marketing, which was originally focused on corporate event planning, but eventually shifted into creative marketing focusing on product development, branding, and positioning. Andy renamed the company Play in 1999 and grew the business significantly over the next decade.

When the opportunity came to sell Play to the global strategic consultancy Prophet in 2008, Andy was intrigued. He sought advice from a long-time mentor and friend, Stan Peterson, who had sold several businesses over his decades-long career, and asked him, *"How do you know if it's the right time to sell?"* Stan replied, *"I always think about selling earlier than others, because a sale provides new chapters for the founder, for the company, and for the employees. Not selling can keep those new chapters from beginning."*

That advice resonated with Andy, who spent the next nine months in a trial courtship with Prophet that culminated in a sale in 2009.

Andy remained with Prophet after the sale and began his second chapter, first as senior partner with Prophet and then later as the firm's Chief Curator and Provocateur. That more expansive role would not have been possible had Play remained independent. The sale also allowed the Play brand to enter a new chapter, expanding with the aid of Prophet into new markets and more interesting clients. Lastly, becoming part of a larger organization created a new chapter for Play's employees, about half of whom are still with Prophet and enjoying their roles within a more expansive firm. The other half of Play's team that has now moved onto new opportunities could do so in part from the new beginning that the sale provided.

Andy left Prophet in 2014 to start his third chapter, which has included publishing a best-selling book, *Look at More: A Proven Approach to Innovation, Growth, and Change,* as well as working as an advisor to C-suite executives of Fortune 100 companies and advising and investing in private equity-backed mid-cap companies.

For Andy, it all goes back to that advice he received from his mentor. *"It was great vision on Stan's part to say do it earlier than you think and do it to challenge yourself, your brand, and your team."*

\* \* \*

One of the most difficult aspects of a successful exit is determining when to sell. Rarely does an ideal buyer come out of nowhere offering a sweetheart deal, thereby deciding when to exit an easy one. Neither selling too soon, nor holding on too long, is ideal; both yield suboptimal results. The key is recognizing when exit conditions are ideal and your business is at an inflection point where new ownership would have a significant impact on the future growth trajectory.

> The key is recognizing when exit conditions are ideal and your business is at an inflection point where new ownership would have a significant impact on the future growth trajectory.

Often, the signs that the business is ready for a new chapter are there if you know where to look.

## THE ROLE OF A SALE IN THE CORPORATE LIFE CYCLE

High school friends, Kevin Lee and David Chen, had just graduated from the University of Virginia's Darden Business School and were excited about the next chapter in their lives. Having studied computer science while earning their MBAs, the pair had developed a prototype inventory management system that they were eager to put to use in the real world.

This computer program could not only track a company's on-hand inventory, a basic operating necessity, but also used complex algorithms to analyze usage data to predict when quantities of each item dropped to the ideal point of reordering, given lead times and minimum order quantities for that particular Stock Keeping Unit (SKU). In addition, it also made recommendations as to the optimum number of products to purchase with the next order.

Businesses continually work to maintain an optimum balance between reducing the amount of capital invested in inventory while still having enough products on hand to satisfy customer demand. This inventory management program would be a valuable way for business owners to use automation to achieve that balance.

As sons of Chinese immigrant parents who were small retail business owners, Kevin and David had attended business school to pursue their entrepreneurial dream of building a business of their own. *"We knew we lacked some of the skills needed to get a company off the ground,"* recalls David, *"so we thought an MBA would fill in the gaps in our skill sets."*

Not only did an MBA give them a well-rounded education on all facets of running a business, the inventory management system they developed was a bonus.

Kevin says, *"We didn't necessarily want to create a software company based on our program, but instead, we wanted to use our software as a competitive advantage within an operating business."* So, the two budding entrepreneurs set out to find an opportunity to start a business that would benefit from their proprietary software.

Knowing that distributors of imported goods relied heavily on in-stock inventory, the pair believed a business in that sector would have the most to gain from their inventory management platform. So, they started looking for growing niche end markets that relied on imported products.

After several months, Kevin and David settled on the outpatient cosmetic surgery market and decided to first focus on the durable medical equipment (DME) that practitioners use during exams and treatment. Rather than import the standard equipment for distribution, they saw an opportunity to enter the market with a better version of one of the basic pieces of equipment and set to work on improving the industry-standard design. Kevin and David found a factory to build their new products and worked with industrial designers to create a prototype, which they introduced to the US market with a small booth at a major cosmetic surgery industry trade show.

The market loved the redesigned equipment, and orders soon started pouring in. *"In the first few years,"* the pair remembered, *"everything was running so smoothly. Our program worked terrifically for managing inventory, and we were selling products as fast as our factory could produce them."*

Based on the initial success of the first debut product and the customer relationships they built, the pair expanded their offering to include many of the consumable supplies that these clinics also needed. They saw a tremendous opportunity to be a one-stop shop for the cosmetic surgery industry. But as their product offering expanded, so did the complexity of managing the business.

Within six months of introducing the consumables line, problems started popping up from all sides. Managing numerous international vendors with several hundred SKUs was much harder than the early days of one factory with only a handful of items. The breadth of the product offering overwhelmed the inventory management software, and customer orders were shipping late. Some of the company's most popular products were even facing significant backorders. And the company's fast sales growth created a strain on cash flow, as more and more money was needed to fund higher levels of working capital.

Most importantly, the partners realized the business was growing beyond their management expertise. *"We got to the point where we knew we needed outside help to take the business forward,"* Kevin said. *"Our choice was to scale back to a more manageable size or bring in new partners to help us take it to the next level."* Scaling back would have made the business easier to manage, but it also would have meant discontinuing several major product categories that would have been costly and hurt the company's hard-earned reputation with its customers. It also would have capped the company's growth, making it difficult for the business to retain talent and increase in value over time.

On the other hand, bringing on a new partner meant selling a portion of the company's equity to an investor, who could then help the company continue its growth trajectory. Partnering with a private equity firm would enable the founders to cash in on the company's success to-date, creating substantial personal wealth, while retaining a portion of the equity going forward to also benefit from future growth. While the idea of giving up control was initially difficult to swallow, the partners ultimately decided the combination of receiving a substantial amount of cash that would provide financial security for their family, attracting a partner to help address the operational concerns, and still retaining a portion, albeit smaller, of a faster-growing company was the best path forward.

With that goal in mind, Kevin and David engaged an investment bank to help find a private equity partner for the business. With $7 million in earnings, a robust M&A market, and the company's cosmetic surgery end market growing nicely at 5–6 percent per year, their investment bankers confirmed that this was a good time to market the business.

While some PE groups were uncertain about investing in the cosmetic surgery sector given its history of malpractice suits and the limited size of the addressable market, several private equity firms saw the company as a diamond-in-the-rough opportunity. One group was not only comfortable investing in the sector, but saw tremendous potential to consolidate the fragmented cosmetic surgery supply sector. That firm struck a deal to buy 80 percent of the company from the founders, who retained 20 percent of the equity in the business going forward.

After the transaction closed, improvements started occurring in rapid fashion. *"It was as if rescuers had arrived on the scene, and a new level of professionalism permeated the company,"* David said. As part of the planned transition, the PE firm brought in a new CEO, VP of Sales, and VP of Supply Chain Management, while Kevin and David stepped back to roles on the company's Board of Directors. Utilizing the skills of the more experienced management team, the operational challenges melted away within the first year. While the company's executive team was focused internally, the new PE owner conducted a buy-side search within the industry and identified three smaller competitors with attractive products and customers that were ready to sell. Over their three years of ownership, the PE firm acquired all three of these businesses, doubling the size of the company's revenue. That, coupled with the higher margins gained through operational improvements made by the new management team, led to a tripling of the company's profits over the same period.

With all these accomplishments, the PE firm decided it was time to sell in order to realize a return on their investment. They hired a well-known middle-market investment bank to run a broad M&A auction process, and when the company was sold to a larger PE firm, the founders and their PE partner had made four times their invested capital in just three years. *"We couldn't believe it,"* Kevin exclaimed, *"because of the improvements that occurred under the PE firm's ownership, we ended up making more money selling our last 20 percent than we did when we sold our first 80 percent."* In addition to the economic reward, the partners were proud that the business that they initially had created as a start-up after grad school was now a sustainable and vibrant company well-positioned for long-term growth.

**OPTIMAL TIMING TO SELL**

Deciding to sell all or even a part of one's business is an important decision that takes significant planning and deliberation. The success that Kevin and David experienced resulted from two well-timed exits. In both cases, we can see that if they had decided to sell significantly earlier or later, it would likely have yielded a less attractive outcome.

Let's take their first exit. If they had decided to sell earlier, they would likely have been too small to attract interest from private equity investors, which have minimum thresholds for revenue or earnings. While some PE firms will invest in businesses with as little as $1–2 million in earnings, most require at least $5 million. If they had waited too long, on the other hand, the challenges facing the business would have hurt its financial performance, resulting in declining results that would have scared off most private equity firms. The only ones that would have remained interested would have been value buyers looking for out-of-favor companies at discount valuations.

Given the importance of timing on the success of a sale process, how can business owners know when the time is right?

I counsel prospective clients that, when considering the opportune time to sell their company, they should evaluate three conditions. The health of the M&A markets, the outlook for your industry, and the state of your company's performance all influence the receptivity your business will receive in the marketplace. My advice is if all three are strong, or at least two of the three are strong and the third is neutral, it is likely a good time to sell.

Let's consider each of these in turn.

### M&A MARKET ACTIVITY

First, the volume of M&A transactions should be healthy. Like selling a house in a hot real estate market, business owners should sell when M&A activity is strong. The more buyers there are looking for deals, the better your business will be received.

At the time of this publishing in 2020, middle-market deal activity is currently at record levels, fueled by cheap debt and an overabundance of private equity capital that must be invested in private companies. Mergers and acquisitions activity in the US has been at historically record levels since 2014. According to industry data-source PitchBook, approximately 111,800 companies were sold in North America from 2009–2018, with 12,661 changing hands in 2018 alone for an aggregate $2.4 trillion. By comparison, there were only 8,705 M&A transactions in 2010, totaling $1.0 trillion in value.[8]

Private equity groups are one of the primary drivers of M&A activity. These firms raise pools of capital from pension funds, endowments, and other institutional investors, and then use that capital to acquire private companies. They then work with the management teams of those companies to grow and improve the businesses, with an eye toward selling them for a profit within three to five years.

Once a PE firm raises a new fund, they are under pressure to invest that capital in private businesses. Most PE funds have an overall life span of seven to ten years from the time a new fund is raised until all the capital needs to be returned to the investors. If the hold period for one of their portfolio companies averages five years, or more in some cases, they need to make their initial investments within the first several years after raising the fund. PitchBook reports that private equity firms raised over $195 billion in new funds in 2018

---

8    (PitchBook Data, Inc. 2019)

alone,[9] and all that capital will need to be invested over the next several years.

This supply of PE money searching for new acquisition opportunities, coupled with plenty of debt financing at historically inexpensive rates and corporate buyers also competing for acquisition targets, is fueling a sellers' market that shows no signs of slowing.

### INDUSTRY OUTLOOK

The outlook for the company's industry should be positive. It is always better to sell when your industry is in favor and buoyed by strong growth fundamentals. Do you participate in an industry experiencing headwinds or tailwinds? Is it growing or shrinking; the wave of the future or an echo of past glory days? Just as a rising tide lifts all boats, so too does a favorable industry raise the valuations of its participating companies.

The inverse of that adage holds true as well; a receding tide lowers all boats. It is difficult to receive a premium valuation for a business performing well in a strong M&A environment but operates in an industry that is out of favor. Buyers will be concerned that industry headwinds will be working against whatever growth the company may otherwise generate, like trying to swim against a strong current. You may make some forward progress, but it will be much harder than it needs to be, and you just might get swept away.

---

9    (PitchBook Data, Inc. 2019)

All industries can face headwinds that lead to periods of being out of favor. Shifts in trade policies, such as quotas and tariffs, can impact businesses that rely on imports or exports to grow. Industries driven by consumer preferences or commodities like steel or oil can swing in and out of favor over time. Segments of the economy reliant on government funding, such infrastructure construction companies, go through boom and bust cycles driven by the passage or expiration of funding bills. Even regulatory changes, such as in healthcare reimbursement or tax policies, can significantly influence a sector's outlook.

For example, I once had a client who ran a boutique consulting firm that advised clients on how to maximize the research and development tax credits they could receive from state and federal governments for their projects. During much of the debate leading up to the overhaul of the US tax code in 2017, the tax credits and incentives that the company relied on helping their clients receive were scheduled to be eliminated. Fortunately for my client, the tax credits were only modestly impacted by the final tax code, but had they been eliminated as discussed, my client's industry would have been wholly unattractive to outside buyers.

**COMPANY INFLECTION POINT**
Lastly, the company's recent historical financial performance and the near-term outlook should be robust. Remember that buyers are buying the future, not the past, and they will look to a company's recent performance to validate their assumptions about how that company is likely to perform under their ownership.

This one is perhaps the toughest to objectively assess, as you want to bring your company to market when it is hitting its stride. Ideally, the financial metrics of growth and profitability have been strong and improving for the past several years, and the company is posting solid year-over-year growth. You definitely want the outlook for the next several years to be bright. If your business has peaked and is plateauing or even starting to decline, you will be approaching buyers from a position of weakness and your company's valuation will suffer.

Most importantly, buyers love finding companies that are at an inflection point in their life cycle, and this is often when we see multiple competing bidders that drive valuations significantly higher than otherwise expected. Companies are at an inflection point when they have been performing well and have significant growth opportunities ahead of them but face some near-term challenges to capitalizing on those opportunities. Private equity groups love when the lack of capital is at the root of that near-term obstacle that stands between the status quo and unlocking significant growth, since they have lots of capital to invest.

Examples of inflection points include the need for significant capital investment, such as adding a new multimillion-dollar production line or opening a second production facility. It can also mean buying out inactive shareholders who are holding the company back or funding a large new order of inventory to expand the company's product line. Having the opportunity to acquire a competitor or expand into a new geography through acquisitions are also examples of inflection points that private equity groups excel at addressing.

Inflection points can also exist when a company's founder has reached the point where their company has grown beyond their management expertise. The success that Kevin and David experienced hinged on this important principle. They were brutally honest with themselves about when their company had reached a point where it exceeded their capabilities. This conclusion is often hard for founders to acknowledge. But admitting they weren't the best leaders of their business from a certain point forward freed Kevin and David to find a partner to fill in the gaps, which enabled the business to reach new heights significantly more financially rewarding than if they'd tried to continue on their own.

\* \* \*

Exiting your business is an important milestone in the life of the owner, the business, and its employees. New ownership with fresh capital and strategic resources can usher in a new chapter in a company's evolution, providing new opportunities. As you consider the all-important decision of when to exit your business, you'll be wise to consider the state of the M&A market, your industry, and your business. If at least two of the three are positive, it is probably a great time to consider an exit.

In the following chapter, we'll look at the next steps you'll take once you are ready to move forward with a sale process. We'll review what a three-stage auction process looks like and the various types of M&A advisors that will serve as your guide to ensure you achieve the best outcome possible.

## ACTION ITEMS

- **Look outward.** Look into the current health of the M&A market to see how active it is. An M&A advisor can offer free insights into M&A activity overall and within your industry sector (we'll learn more about them in the next chapter). Assess the health of your industry and grade its outlook. Are you seeing consolidation or other M&A activity within your industry and among your competitors? If so, it may indicate that the external conditions are optimal for a sale.

- **Look inward.** Take a step back and strategically evaluate where your business is in its corporate evolution and where you are in terms of having the energy and expertise needed to lead it forward. Is the company reaching an inflection point where new ownership could shift the business into a higher gear? Are some opportunities not being pursued for lack of capital, expertise, or talent? Consider what new chapters a sale would bring for you, for the company, and for your employees.

# PART 2

# KICKING OFF
# THE M&A PROCESS

# CHAPTER 5

# ENGAGE
# AN M&A ADVISOR

———

Colette Anderson is the former CEO and managing partner of NT Brands, the parent company of a portfolio of premium consumer brands in several active lifestyle categories. One of the biggest successes of her twenty-year career at NT Brands was the lucrative sale of one of the company's fastest-growing divisions, McIntire Industries.

Colette personally championed the idea of selling McIntire to her Board of Directors, who were initially wary of divesting one of NT Brands' most profitable and fast-growing divisions. Colette convinced the Board that given some preliminary interest that several potential buyers had expressed, it was at least worth seeing what offers might be out there. With the Board's tentative blessing, Colette set about entertaining offers for McIntire. Yet it took two failed attempts on Colette's part over several wasted months before a new approach yielded what was ultimately a successful outcome.

Like many business owners, Colette believed that she could sell McIntire on her own, without wasting money on hiring an investment bank. After all, she knew McIntire better than anyone, and she had been approached at industry trade shows over the past few years by several well-known private equity groups interested in buying McIntire. In addition, she didn't want to unnecessarily alarm McIntire's executives or other employees by telling them about a potential sale until it was certain to close. So why not put together some high-level information about the company, approach the groups that had already expressed interest, and see what they had to say?

With this thought in mind, Colette enlisted the help of NT Brands' COO, and without including anyone from within the McIntire division, began pulling together the information needed to draft a Confidential Information Memorandum (CIM), the descriptive document that Colette would share with potential buyers. When the CIM was complete, Colette scheduled meetings to present the McIntire opportunity in-person to Lamda Capital and Omega Partners, the two most aggressive private equity firms who had approached them several times in the past about selling. Both potential buyers were interested in the opportunity, and shortly after the meetings with Colette, each submitted similar preliminary offers for McIntire at attractive valuation ranges.

The NT Brands Board was thrilled with the response from the potential buyers and fully supported Colette's recommendation to proceed with Lamda Capital, which based on the two initial meetings, she believed represented the best fit for McIntire. After more than a month of due diligence work, though, the deal hit a serious roadblock.

Having only spent time with Colette, Lamda Capital made their offer contingent on her leaving NT Brands to run McIntire for them post-closing, which had never been part of Colette's plan. On the contrary, she saw a significant opportunity for her to continue leading NT Brands after selling the McIntire division and had plans to use the proceeds from the sale to expand NT Brands' international presence. When Colette told the buyer that, while the current leadership team at McIntire would remain with the business post-closing, she herself would be staying with the parent, Lamda Capital rescinded their offer and dropped out of the process.

Undeterred, Colette approached Omega Partners and restarted the closing diligence process with them. Unfortunately, the same issue arose several weeks into diligence. Like the first buyer, Omega Partners also wanted Colette to run the business, and when they learned she would remain with NT Brands post-closing, they too rescinded their offer and dropped out.

Colette and the NT Brands Board members were excited about the valuation levels that both buyers had provided, but knew that approaching additional buyers in the same way would not be productive. They needed an M&A expert to help them navigate the overall process, including having a plan to proactively address Colette's remaining with NT Brands after the divestiture. So, they invited three well-respected investment banks with experience selling consumer products companies to submit proposals to represent McIntire in an M&A process. While each of the investment banks made compelling cases for their respective firms to be selected, a clear favorite emerged based on fit with the team, and NT Brands retained Dexter Stephens & Co. to sell McIntire.

During the project's kick-off meeting with the DS&Co. team, Colette shared the CIM she had drafted and relayed to them the failed experience with the two previous buyers. The DS&Co. Managing Director on the deal team responded, *"The reason your processes failed wasn't the CIM that you drafted, and it wasn't the business itself. It was because private equity firms aren't going to run the business. They want to back a team, and you're not presenting a team. You're only presenting you."* In other words, by keeping the process under wraps and not including the senior McIntire team, Colette was unintentionally putting herself forward as the leader of the division in the eyes of potential buyers. When buyers learned that she was never planning to remain with McIntire, the PE firms dropped out because they had not met the team that would lead the company under their ownership.

The DS&Co. bankers set to work creating a more fulsome CIM using the one Colette created as a starting point, and she confidentially enlisted the involvement of the top four executives at McIntire: its President, CFO, Head of Sales, and Head of Product Development. With their additional expertise, the new CIM provided a much more detailed view of McIntire than the previous one had. When the time came to have initial meetings with buyers after first-round bids were received, the four McIntire executives delivered the presentations to the potential suitors, with Colette in the background only to answer questions from the parent company's perspective.

This approach yielded dramatically better results. DS&Co. received multiple final offers for McIntire that were higher than those from the earlier failed process, and with DS&Co.'s four-person team of investment bankers' providing significant bandwidth to handle buyers' requests for detailed information, McIntire moved forward from a position of strength with multiple competing bidders simultaneously. This strategy ensured that if one buyer stumbled in the process and tried to lower the price, other buyers were still in play. The transaction ultimately closed in a sale to a large international PE firm at a purchase price that represented a significant premium to the initial offers and the Board's expectations.

> This strategy ensured that if one buyer stumbled in the process and tried to lower the price, other buyers were still in play. The transaction ultimately closed in a sale to a large international PE firm at a purchase price that represented a significant premium to the initial offers and the Board's expectations.

DS&Co. served many functions during the process, including producing a detailed CIM, contacting a broader group of potential buyers than Colette could have alone, and coordinating the overall process. In addition, DS&Co. ensured that the high volume of due diligence information that buyers requested was accurate and tied together appropriately. This is a service that sellers often undervalue. *"Buyers will come in and just crawl into every detail of the business over the past three to four years, and they want every piece of informa-tion, sliced and diced twelve different ways,"* Colette recalls. *"Having DS&Co. to manage and provide quality control on all of the information requests was one of the many valuable roles they played in our sale process."* Having the negotiating strength of multiple interested parties is wasted if they later drop out because the seller can't provide timely and accurate answers to their litany of information requests.

As she reflects on the overall sales process, including the two false starts, Colette learned a valuable lesson. *"Selling McIntire was the hardest thing I ever did. Building the business from zero to roughly $100 million was far easier than selling it. I should never have tried to go it alone."* She experienced firsthand how difficult it is to try to sell your business on your own. Only through engaging an M&A adviser and running a competitive auction process could the successful outcome be achieved.

* * *

## THE IMPORTANCE OF HIRING AN M&A ADVISOR

An M&A advisory firm provides value to its clients in numerous and often overlooked ways that will ultimately yield higher purchase prices than owners could achieve on their own. These advisors are the driving force in moving the M&A process forward, from beginning to end, and serve as your advocate all along the way. They create the necessary process documents, identify potential buyers, and serve as your ambassador to the market of potential buyers. M&A advisors also liaison with your M&A attorney and any other members of your M&A team, ensuring smooth coordination and no miscommunications internally. M&A advisors work exclusively with their clients, so you'll commit to working with only the firm you select for a certain period, typically eighteen months.

From a fee standpoint, M&A advisors charge a retainer (a one-time up-front or monthly recurring fee) at the start of an engagement, and a larger success fee tied to the sale price that only becomes due if a transaction closes. The retainer is the only fee you are committing to if for some reason a deal doesn't occur. The success fee paid to an M&A advisor increases with higher deal values and is thus designed to align their incentives with yours. Given this industry-standard fee structure and their ability to run controlled auction processes that maximize the sellers' negotiating leverage, M&A advisors generate incremental sale proceeds from buyers that more than cover the cost of their fee. In other words, a good M&A advisor will pay for themselves many times over by delivering a higher sale price than you would have otherwise received on your own, more than defraying the cost of their fees.

Let's look briefly at the valuable role that M&A advisors play during each of the three main phases of the process: Preparation, Marketing, and Closing.

**PHASE I: PREPARATION**
M&A advisors understand how to present their client's business to potential buyers in the best possible way. Starting with your in-depth, detailed knowledge of your company, M&A

advisors can create a compelling marketing document based on their years of experience. Knowing what information to include in the CIM and how to position the company is as much art as science. The trick is providing enough specificity in the CIM to create interest with potential buyers without sharing too much sensitive, confidential information too early in the process. Generating excitement in the market that will drive higher valuations for your business comes from presenting your company as a compelling story of opportunity, not simply the facts and figures.

> Generating excitement in the market that will drive higher valuations for your business comes from presenting your company as a compelling story of opportunity, not simply the facts and figures.

Buyers are most interested in what is possible for the company under their ownership, so it is important to paint a realistic vision of growth and strength. At the same time, buyers will expect a base of certain facts, such as the number of employees and size of the operating facility, for example.

In addition to preparing the marketing materials, M&A advisors help their clients determine what types of buyers should be considered for a particular client situation. For example, smaller companies for sale may be attractive to individuals seeking to personally acquire a business that they can continue to operate and grow. Larger companies with several million dollars of earnings may want to consider strategic and financial buyers.

Strategic buyers are corporations in your company's industry or related sectors that may be interested in acquiring your company as part of their strategic growth strategy. Financial buyers, including private equity groups and the investing offices of wealthy families, are attractive buyers for companies that have a strong management team in place looking for a partner to help them grow their company faster than they could otherwise. We'll delve more deeply into the topic of potential buyers in Chapter 8.

After considering your situation and determining the appropriate types of acquirers to include, your M&A advisors will then conduct research to compile a list of specific potential buyers that will be contacted in the next phase of the process.

### PHASE II: MARKETING
Once the CIM and List of Potential Purchasers are complete, your M&A advisor will contact the approved buyers on your behalf, typically using a no-names one-page "teaser" to get their attention. If buyers are interested in learning more about the company after reviewing the teaser, they must sign a nondisclosure agreement before receiving the CIM.

After the buyers spend a few weeks with the CIM, the M&A advisor requests first-round bids, called initial indications of interest, on a certain date from all interested buyers. From these IOIs, you and your advisor can see how the various buyers are valuing the company and decide which buyers will be invited to the next round of management meetings.

It is important to note that in this type of process, no listing price or other predetermined offering price is used by the advisor. Instead, a consistent set of information is provided to all buyers on the same timeline. The market determines the company value.

The second stage of the marketing phase involves holding face-to-face meetings with each of the selected buyers from the first round. These meetings are important ways for both parties to learn more, essentially serving as a two-way interview. Potential buyers will be interested in meeting your management team and hearing more about your plans for the business. At the same time, you will want to interview each buyer to understand what is driving their interest in your company and how they see the business operating post-closing. These three- to four-hour meetings are typically held over the course of two to three weeks and include a tour of the company's facility, which can occur after hours if necessary.

Assuming the meeting goes well and both sides want to move forward, each buyer is provided access to an online repository of more detailed company information, reports, records, and filings. Buyers and their functional diligence providers, such as accounting, insurance, and legal advisors, review the information in the online data room to complete enough diligence to submit a formal offer for the business, called a Letter of Intent, by the deadline set by the M&A advisor. Your M&A advisor will present the LOIs to you and develop a negotiating plan with one or more of the top bidders. They'll represent you in negotiating the best outcome among the final parties. The marketing phase ends when you execute the winning bidder's LOI, granting them exclusivity in the transaction for the time needed to close.

**PHASE III: CLOSING**

The closing process comprises a final due diligence and legal documentation. At this point, you have agreed to the deal in principle and want to close the transaction on the agreed-upon terms as quickly as possible. Delays here will only work against you, giving more time for some unforeseen issue to arise. Your M&A advisor will coordinate the vast amount of due diligence information that the buyer and its advisors will want to review. At this stage, essentially anything they want to review is fair game, though your advisor will push back on requests outside industry norms. Without their setting boundaries, you could drown in a never-ending cycle of diligence requests as the buyer strives to turn over every possible rock before closing.

As final diligence winds down and any issues the buyer discovered are resolved through negotiation, attorneys for both sides begin drafting and negotiating the definitive legal agreement that will govern the transaction, called a Purchase & Sale Agreement (PSA). These documents are typically fifty or more pages with dozens of supporting schedules and cover all aspects of the transaction, from what exactly is being acquired by the buyer (likely not the family heirloom in your office lobby) to what recourse the buyer has if some unforeseen problem arises in the months after closing.

Representing your interest in this process should be an attorney with specific experience in M&A transactions, not your general counsel or real estate attorney. M&A attorneys know the pitfalls to avoid and what market terms are for the myriad of negotiated points within the PSA. Like M&A advisors, good M&A attorneys are well worth their fee. If you don't have a good law firm, your M&A advisor can offer several recommendations.

When the PSA and supporting schedules are finalized and executed, the transaction closes. This means legal ownership transfers to the buyer, and the purchase price, net of outstanding expenses, is wired into your bank account. While there will still be some loose ends to tie up in the coming months, you can breathe a sigh of relief and celebrate a successful exit.

## SELECTING THE RIGHT M&A ADVISOR

M&A advisors come in many shapes and sizes. To help find the perfect one for you, let's look at some of the types of firms that offer M&A services.

### BUSINESS BROKERS

For smaller businesses valued below $2–3 million, business brokers are the best choice of M&A advisor. They help their clients assemble a brief sales overview of the company and solicit potential buyers by posting the opportunity (on a no-names basis) on their website and online business exchanges, such as BizBuySell.com. Rather than running an auction process, business brokers set a list price for their client's business and negotiate with interested buyers as they surface. Most communities across the country have local independent or franchised business brokers; as with all professional services firms, check references on both the firm and individual broker you'll be working with before signing on the dotted line.

### INVESTMENT BANKS

Investment banks sell businesses valued from several million dollars to those worth billions. These firms offer clients a full-service approach to running a comprehensive M&A auction process designed to efficiently canvass the market and drive the best possible outcome. Investment banks will assign a team of three to five professionals, led by a Managing Director and including junior staff, to each project. A word of caution: many clients mistakenly select an investment bank based on the qualifications of the firm, rather than the more important and relevant qualifications of the individual members assigned to your deal. It pays to understand the expertise and strengths of your *deal team* when choosing an investment bank, rather than those of the overall firm.

> It pays to understand the expertise and strengths of your deal team when choosing an investment bank, rather than those of the overall firm.

The first criteria to select an investment bank is transaction size. Though the exact size delineations are murky, the investment banking world is segmented into three groups: bulge bracket firms (specializing in deals valued at over $1 billion), middle-market firms (deals from $100 million to $1 billion), and lower middle market firms (deals under $100 million). Larger deals are typically more complex and require larger deal teams, thus generating larger fees.

Firms also gain experience within the ecosystem of likely buyers, lenders, and service providers in their respective deal size ranges. As such, a bulge bracket investment bank like Goldman Sachs wouldn't be a good choice for a $25 million deal, nor would a lower middle-market firm be for a $2 billion sale transaction. Only consider investment banking firms that fit the size of your business.

Another distinguishing characteristic of the investment banking landscape is a firm's approach to industry specialization. Some firms will work exclusively on transactions in one or more industry verticals, such as health care, business services, or consumer goods, while others staunchly maintain an industry-generalist approach.

Specialist firms will tell you they are more effective because they develop deep domain expertise in industry-specific trends, buyers, and deal-structuring nuances. Generalist firms will counter that they take a fresh approach to each client assignment, avoiding the complacency that can develop by specialists accustomed to calling the same buyers on every transaction, and that a well-run M&A process (not industry expertise) is what really matters in driving the best outcome.

My advice is to use an industry specialist if you operate in an unusually complex or highly regulated industry, such as banking or technology. Otherwise, it is more of personal preference; meet with firms from both categories and pick the best option for you. Beyond deal size and industry specialization, you may want to include the size and location of the investment bank in your selection criteria. The size spectrum ranges from large firms with hundreds of bankers in dozens of offices across the country and around the world to single-office boutique firms.

> Beyond deal size and industry specialization, you may want to include the size and location of the investment bank in your selection criteria. The size spectrum ranges from large firms with hundreds of bankers in dozens of offices across the country and around the world to single-office boutique firms.

I know of no correlation between the size of the firm and the quality of representation; this is largely a personal preference. Similarly, some clients prefer working with a firm that has a local presence, making in-person meetings easier to schedule and reducing travel costs, which are passed along to the client in the form of reimbursable expenses. Others prefer to use an out-of-town firm as an added precautionary measure against confidentiality breaches.

## SENSE OF URGENCY

One of the most overlooked benefits of engaging an M&A advisor is the sense of urgency they bring to the transaction. While you still have a business to run during the process, with all its inherent distractions and responsibilities, your exit process is your advisor's sole focus. It is their "day job," and their focus can keep the momentum from lagging. As one senior M&A advisor learned all too well, sometimes a seemingly inconsequential single extra day over the course of a multiyear sale process can mean the difference between a successful closing and major setback.

* * *

The news coming out of Honduras and the surrounding countries was bleak. Hurricane Mitch had developed into a Category 5 hurricane and was hitting Central America with overwhelming force. Though it paled in comparison to the devastation that occurred in the region, the impact of the second-deadliest Atlantic hurricane in history was also being felt well outside the storm's radius in a sleek Boston conference room.

*"How could we have let ourselves get to this point?"* Mike Papile wondered. He and his team of investment bankers were on the eve of closing the sale of five manufacturing facilities located in several Central American countries. Though all the paperwork and funding were in place and ready for tomorrow's exchange, there was a major problem. One of the largest plants being sold, a components factory on the coast of Honduras directly in the path of the storm, was offline, and no one knew its status. The buyer had just notified Mike's

team that they would not be closing the transaction until the condition of all the factories could be verified, jeopardizing a deal that had been over two years in the making.

Exasperated at having fallen short so close to the finish line, Mike stared out the window of his firm's conference room as the sun set on a beautiful fall day in Boston. *"If we had cut out just twelve hours from the process somewhere over the past thirty months, this deal would have closed without a hitch. Now the deal is on hold as the impact of Mitch is determined."*

\* \* \*

Business owners should take as much time as they need to decide when the time is right to sell their company. But once that decision is made, the entire cadence of the process needs to completely change. A heightened sense of urgency must permeate the sale process and everyone involved in it, led by the business owner and their M&A advisor. Nothing good comes from a deal process dragging out longer than it should. With additional time comes the chance that something unforeseen will pop up to derail the transaction, interrupt the momentum, or cause the buyer to walk away. These events can be internal, such as badly missing a month's financial budget, or external like the passing of new government regulations that make your business less profitable. But in all cases, you'll have wished the deal had closed beforehand and, short of a time machine, you'll be powerless to avoid the consequences.

The most compelling example of this happened to Mike Papile, a managing director at the Boston-based boutique investment bank, Covington Associates. In his mid-fifties with a broad smile and a firm handshake, Mike has spent over thirty years advising privately held, publicly traded, and family-owned businesses. He has assisted them in evaluating their strategic alternatives, raising capital, and executing M&A transactions.

Mike had a client that was considering selling some of its manufacturing facilities in Central America that were no longer central to their strategic focus. This multibillion international conglomerate had created over several decades a division that manufactured specialized packaging used to get their products from the field to supermarket shelves. To reduce transportation costs, the plants were located close to the plantations that grew the crops that their packaging supported, often in extremely remote rural areas. Over the years, the factories had expanded into making packaging and other consumer goods for third-party customers, in addition to supplying its parent company with the packaging it needed.

In late 1995, Mike's firm was engaged to complete a strategic review of the division and determine how it would be received by the market should the parent carve it off. Mike and his team completed the analysis, which indicated that the manufacturing network was worth more to a new buyer than to its existing owners and thus should be sold. *"Given the enormous size of our client and the complexity of its internal bureaucracy,"* Mike notes, *"we saw that it was taking longer than it should to get us the information we needed to complete the strategic review. We knew we'd be fighting this sluggishness throughout the sale process."* Even after the clear recommendation to sell the divisions was completed and presented to the Board early the following year, the client took weeks to give Mike's team the green light to take the operation to market.

Right from the start, the process was plagued by setbacks and delays. *"What should have taken us six to nine months turned into two years,"* Mike remembers. Largely driven by the lack of prioritization of the project by the conglomerate's internal team and the inability of the IT systems to generate the information that would be needed by buyers, Mike's team pushed the process forward, though it often felt like they were fighting some unseen force of resistance. By the fall, however, Mike's team had struck a deal in principle with a buyer for all five plants and could feel the finish line just around the corner. Closing was set for October 31, and all substantive work by the buyer was finished, all open issues resolved, and funding was ready to be wired to the seller.

Then, news of Hurricane Mitch's forming in the Caribbean Sea threw all the closing preparations into disarray. The storm hit landfall on October 29, and the client's Honduran plant went offline soon thereafter. Located in a remote area of the jungle down a single dirt access road, the condition of this production facility, which was the second largest of the five being sold, was unknown. Fearing the plant had been destroyed, the buyer called off the closing for the following day, reaching Mike and his team in the Boston conference room.

As days turned into weeks and the significant damage to the plant was better understood, the buyer agreed to move forward and close the transaction, but for only the four plants that remained operational and for a purchase price of millions less than originally agreed.

Over twenty years later, Mike tells that story to each of his new clients at the start of their M&A process. *"If we had cut out twelve hours from the process at some point over that two-year process and closed the transaction before the plant was hit by the storm, we would have achieved a vastly more attractive outcome for our client."* Ever since, Mike works daily to push his deals forward. *"I won't schedule a call on a Monday if we can squeeze it in on a Friday afternoon,"* he notes. *"A day or two lost here or there, then a week when a key person is out on vacation, all have a snowball effect."* Over the course of a process, even minor periodic delays can accumulate to delay the process a month or more.

In that extra time, you just never know what may happen that could derail the transaction. It doesn't have to be the deadliest hurricane in over 200 years, but it could be losing a key customer or employee, receiving notice of a workplace safety audit, or one of a million other unforeseen internal or external events. We'll talk more about these in Chapter 10. Whatever it is, though, its impact could have been neutralized had you and your M&A advisor maintained a sense of urgency throughout the process and closed the transaction before it occurred.

\* \* \*

As we learned from Colette's experience, M&A advisors play an invaluable role in maximizing the sale of your business. Rather than try to negotiate the sale of your company on your own, you will dramatically increase your chances of success by engaging an expert to represent you through the transaction. Once you hire your advisor, follow their lead, including around building and maintaining momentum and a sense of urgency to ensure no stumbling blocks arise that could have been avoided by closing more quickly.

In the next chapter, we'll delve more deeply into one of the most powerful value-creation parts of the process: preparation. Being exceptionally well-prepared before the first contact is made to a potential buyer is critically important to moving the process forward expeditiously and to setting a tone of professionalism that will impress your potential buyers.

### ACTION ITEM

- *Engage an expert.* When you sell your company, use an M&A advisor; they more than pay for themselves and yield significantly better results than going it alone. Next, only consider firms that focus on your company's transaction size and have an impeccable reputation, as they will represent your company to the market. Then make your final selection based on spending time with the specific professionals who will be staffed on your deal and ask questions of them. Do they have experience with similar transactions? Do they have available capacity and aren't spread too thin on too many simultaneous projects? Will senior team members be active throughout the process or disappear after landing you as a client and hand you off to junior staff? Most importantly, do you trust the people on the team?

# CHAPTER 6

# PREPARE AHEAD OF TIME

———

First-time sellers are often surprised by the amount of work that needs to be completed at the beginning of an M&A process. Having labored over the decision to sell their business for months or even years, once the decision is made, they expect buyers to be contacted and the process to begin in earnest. They think that the hard part is deciding to sell. Once they've decided, they think they're ready to roll.

It's not just them. Even private equity firms, whose business it is to buy, improve, and then sell private companies, are tempted to take shortcuts in the preparation phase in a rush to get to market.

Don't fall into this trap. This strategy is almost always short-sighted and guarantees, in the best case, that problems will arise later in the process, or in the worst case, that the transaction process will fail.

For context, let's review what an M&A transaction entails, as discussed in more detail in Chapter 5. Almost every M&A process led by an investment bank comprises three phases:

1. Preparation
2. Marketing
3. Closing

Although the duration of each can vary depending on how many buyers are being contacted, a good rule of thumb is that each phase lasts roughly two months.

### PHASE I—PREPARATION

The investment banker learns as much as possible about the client's business and drafts the Confidential Information Memorandum (CIM), the descriptive offering document on the company, and the list of prospective purchasers that will be contacted in the process.

### PHASE II—MARKETING

The M&A advisor contacts the approved potential buyers, and those interested in buying the company review the CIM after signing a nondisclosure agreement. From there, an auction process unfolds with multiple rounds of bidding, and additional information is provided to participating buyers as the field narrows. Ultimately, a single buyer is chosen at the end of Phase II.

## PHASE III—CLOSING

The buyer completes its in-depth due diligence review of the target, and the legal transaction documentation is negotiated. Phase III ends with the transaction closing.

## WHY PREPARATION IS SO IMPORTANT

How well sellers prepare for the process in Phase I makes all the difference in how smoothly and quickly Phases II and III proceed, and ultimately how successful the transaction will be.

*So, what does preparing well look like?*

Smart investment bankers will help their clients become exceptionally well organized in Phase I so that once they make the first buyer call to kick off Phase II, they can dictate the timing of the process and drive buyers to move quickly. Preparing in Phase I the data schedules and analyses that buyers will want to review in Phases II and III will make the closing process more efficient. Because it is being prepared *before* buyers ask for it, rather than in response to a request when the clock is ticking, management can take their time to make sure each response is 100 percent accurate and effectively communicates the conclusions that the seller wants to deliver.

Preparing well also means presenting the company's financial results on an adjusted basis to exclude nonrecurring and extraordinary costs that are not representative of the company's ongoing earnings-generating capacity (EGC), thereby increasing the company's earnings base, which, in turn, drives a higher purchase price. A good investment banker can help clients differentiate between adjustments that will be accepted by the market and those that are too aggressive, and if used, will erode trust between buyer and seller. Appendix A presents a representative list of approved EBITDA adjustments.

Let's look at examples on opposing ends of the preparation spectrum to see firsthand how the level of preparation impacts the outcome of a given transaction.

### AGGRESSIVE EBITDA ADJUSTMENTS CAN BACKFIRE

In our first scenario, Company X wants to present as aggressive an earnings base as possible as a tactic to drive higher valuations. So, during the preparation phase, the company's owners hire a top management consulting firm to review the three most recent acquisitions that Company X had closed within the past six months and identify potential cost-saving synergies that could be realized by fully integrating the acquisitions into the parent company.

Though the steps to realize these cost-savings have not yet been taken and significant execution risk still exists, Company X's owners insist on including these pro forma savings in the financial adjustments in the CIM. As a result of these pro forma addbacks, EBITDA increased from an as-reported $10 million to an adjusted $14 million. The owners were excited to have buyers start bidding from an adjusted EBITDA $4 million higher.

The decision to take such an aggressive position with the EBITDA adjustments would ultimately backfire, however. During the initial round of bidding, buyers accepted at face value the $14 million of adjusted EBITDA and applied valuation multiples as high as 10x, or $140 million. Ten buyers were selected to move forward in the process to meet the management team and gain access to more detailed financial information, where they learned that $4 million of the EBITDA they had based their valuation on was not actual earnings, but potential cost-saving synergies.

Feeling like they had been materially misled, four of the buyers dropped out of the process entirely and the other six lowered their bids significantly. Now, their bids were based on the actual EBITDA of $10 million, and they also lowered their multiple to 9x, yielding a $90 million valuation. Of course, the owners of Company X, which based on the first-round bids had been focused on selling the business for $140 million, were not excited about selling for $50 million less than expected. Ultimately, they called off the process because buyers could not meet their valuation expectations, which regrettably were never achievable to begin with.

Our second scenario takes an entirely different approach to preparation. Beginning with the same $10 million of unadjusted EBITDA in the same industry, Company Y's management works with their investment bank to make only a few highly defensible EBITDA adjustments, totaling $1 million and takes the time to build a cache of documentation to support each one. They also think critically about how buyers will view their business, identify areas of their company and business model that may be considered weak, and build mini-presentations to proactively describe how they are addressing each of these weaknesses.

They also work with their investment bankers to create high-level five- to eight-page presentations and supporting analyses to provide depth and commentary on each of the five growth strategies that management discusses in the CIM. When all this information is fully proofed and ready, only then are buyers contacted.

Buyers are equally enthralled with Company Y and bid 10x the adjusted EBITDA of $11 million, or $110 million. During management presentations, the groups are given access to the in-depth presentations on growth and strategies for addressing weaknesses that had been prepared in Phase I. Buyers were impressed with the information, but it also allowed the seller to dictate timing to keep a sense of urgency and forward momentum, as well as easily facilitate multiple competing buyers. The management team gave a great impression to their potential new partners because they didn't need to research answers to questions on these topics while buyers waited for it; they could build it ahead of time when no one was looking over their shoulder.

With solid grounding for pricing and a new level of confidence in the management team inspired by the proactive analyses, several buyers increased their valuation multiple to 11x, or $121 million, and one buyer even offered to close on an expedited basis three weeks earlier than the competing buyers. The transaction successfully closed earlier than expected, even accounting for the extra time invested in

Phase I preparation, at $121 million, significantly higher than Company Y's owners had expected.

\* \* \*

The comparison of outcomes between Company X and Company Y is stark. Both begin with the same level of unadjusted EBITDA in the same industry, yet one ends disappointingly without a sale transaction and the other ends successfully with a completed exit that surpassed valuation expectations. Even more interestingly, both scenarios are based on actual transactions represented by the same investment banker. So, why doesn't everyone choose the second scenario? Why did the same banker run both processes?

The answer is surprisingly simple and stems from the same disconnect between hard work and desired results we see in our personal lives. Why do people struggle to maintain an exercise routine and eat a healthy diet when the research is clear on the positive impact these will have on our quality of life? We don't doubt that the hard work performed today will yield the desired result. The issue is that the work feels hard, the benefit is far off, and there's a chance that we will still get the desired result without putting in the work beforehand.

## THE MORE PREPARATION, THE BETTER

For business owners to prepare well for an M&A process, the first step is knowing how to prepare, what information will be worth the time and effort to create *before* buyers even ask for it. Business owners who have made acquisitions in the past or can put themselves in the shoes of a potential buyer may have a good sense of what information will be valuable for buyers to review. In my experience, these business owners are in the minority, which is where the expertise of an M&A advisor comes in.

Experienced M&A advisors have the hands-on knowledge of their past transactions to know what buyers will need to review during the process before they are satisfied enough to close the transaction. Yes, some buyers do more work and some do less, but eliminating both extremes yields a body of information that 80–90 percent of all buyers will need at some point prior to closing.

The question then becomes, how much of what we know we will eventually need to provide to buyers should we prepare proactively, versus waiting until a potential buyer requests it. Though M&A advisors can influence this decision, it is ultimately up to each individual client to decide. As we saw in our examples, the same investment banker ran both processes, so she was well-aware of the benefits of thorough preparation. What differed, though, was Company X's resistance to preparation in its rush to get to market with an aggressively high, though unsubstantiated, adjusted EBITDA.

While the reasons business owners give to avoid preparation are varied, the following excuses are some that I've heard repeatedly in my over two decades of M&A advisory experience.

- "I'm Too Busy"
- "I Don't Think Buyers Will Ask for That"
- "We Don't Have That Handy"

- "This Will Take Too Much Time"
- "We Should Start as High as Possible"

## "I'M TOO BUSY"

Of course, you are busy. Selling your business, even with the help of an M&A advisor, will require additional time on your part above and beyond your "day job" of running the business. But you won't be any less busy when three buyers make the same request five months into the process and they are counting the days until you can answer their question. At that point, they will be evaluating you and your team not only on the quality of the response, but the timeliness of the answer. How much better will you look when you have the accurate and well-thought-out answer readily available when they ask for it?

## "I DON'T THINK BUYERS WILL ASK FOR THAT"

I hear this one a lot. In fact, I've even heard this one in response to some of my standard information requests at the beginning of a sale process, like sales to top ten (code-named) customers, which is included in virtually every CIM ever produced. So, once we get the base-level of information pulled together that must go into the CIM, the idea that we should produce additional information in readiness for future buyer requests can seem to owners to be too much. I understand. But the response I most often give to this excuse is, "*What information would we want to share with buyers that they may not ask for, but would have the most benefit to us?*" This line of thinking helps address perceived areas of weakness in our business or provides additional support to growth opportunities that keep buyers from discounting the company's forecast, and valuation along with it.

## "WE DON'T HAVE THAT HANDY"

That may indeed be the case, but just because you haven't looked at some aspect of your business in a certain way, doesn't mean it isn't insightful and that one or more buyers won't want to see it. Working with your M&A advisor to brainstorm ways to look at your business, such as profitability by customer, channel, or SKU, is a worthwhile exercise.

Identify what analyses are even possible, then run samples for those that don't require an inordinate amount of work and see what they tell you. If it is something positive, your M&A advisor may want to include it in the CIM. If it shines a light on a weak spot, now you know about it and can be ready to handle it if it should arise later. Contrast this to the alternative, when a buyer is waiting for a report you had only run in response to their request that shows a negative trend you weren't previously aware of. Now you're under the gun to figure out a response.

## "THIS WILL TAKE TOO MUCH TIME"

Closely related to the first "I'm Too Busy" excuse, this one may be the most powerful excuse of all, as it drives to a corollary belief: "we need to get to market ASAP." Several weeks of preparation are already needed to complete the CIM and buyers list that must be done before we can call buyers, now you want us to do more prep work that may or may not ever be needed? What about that all-important sense of urgency?

These are all true, and often this rationale wins the day. The need for urgency and getting in front of buyers trumps the need for extra, optional preparation. My advice here is that while urgency is important, consider what limited pieces of preemptive analysis might justify a few days' delay in contacting buyers. Also, remember that time invested in preparation before contacting buyers will only save time later in the process when buyers make detailed information requests.

### "WE SHOULD START AS HIGH AS POSSIBLE"

This one relates specifically to how aggressive to adjust the EBITDA presented in the CIM. It can be quite tempting to throw in as many adjustments as you can think up, knowing the purchase price could be higher by many multiples thereof. Both Company X and Y included adjustments, so the question is not whether to addback nonrecurring or other extraordinary expenses, but how far you take it. As we saw in the two scenarios, going too far can backfire when you lose credibility with buyers that don't agree with your addbacks and then lower their price or drop out. It also creates unrealistic expectations for the selling shareholders that are later unmet, whereas they most likely would have been more accepting of the same outcome had their expectations been more realistic from the start.

My advice is to lean heavily on the expertise of your M&A advisor and include a modestly aggressive list of addbacks clearly quantified and supported in the CIM. You won't get any additional credit for addbacks you never tried to include, but at the same time, if buyers can clearly follow the logic of the adjustments you are presenting, they won't over penalize you for the ones they choose not to underwrite.

\* \* \*

An M&A process is a tremendous undertaking and often emotionally charged given all that owners have put into building their business. It requires a ton of time and effort, not to mention significant amounts of finesse, to be successful. If executed well, a business exit can be life-changing for the selling owner and their family, so the stakes are high. Given this, you only want to go through the process once, and you'll want to give that singular effort every chance of success. Engage a well-qualified M&A advisor and advocate for being more prepared than the necessary minimum; it will pay off in the long run.

The preparation we've covered here primarily focuses on quantitative topics, such as EBITDA adjustments and analyses of revenue, profitability, and cash flow. In the next chapter, we'll tackle the softer side of preparation, the qualitative aspect of positioning. When strong quantitative preparation is coupled with compelling qualitative positioning, exceptional results occur and your payday can increase by millions of dollars.

**ACTION ITEMS**
- *Fight the urge to rush.* Though some or all of the excuses in this chapter may come to you, resist them. Make up your mind to be proactive, to be well-prepared, to be ahead of the game when you complete Phase I and start

contacting buyers. Critically analyze your business from a hypothetical buyer's perspective and think about what data you would like to review to really understand what is happening with your company. What areas of the business model may seem weak or risky to an outside party at first glance? What metrics do you track that give you comfort in those areas? Having a repository of analyses handy to provide to buyers proactively or immediately upon request will increase your professional credibility and keep the process momentum high.

- *Take an appropriately aggressive approach to EBITDA adjustments.* Avoid the temptation to overdo making adjustments to your company's EBITDA. A desire to maximize the purchase price must be balanced against maintaining credibility and goodwill with the buyer, who at some point before closing will go through every EBITDA adjustment in excruciating detail and will make their own determination about which are acceptable versus too aggressive. Appendix A provides a sample list of acceptable EBITDA adjustments you can use to guide your thinking here. Make sure you have supporting documentation for each one ready for buyer confirmation later.

# CHAPTER 7

# USE POSITIONING TO YOUR ADVANTAGE

———

Positioning is one of the most powerful and yet most underutilized tools that business owners have at their disposal when selling their company. How you describe what your company does, as well as the size and definition of the market in which it operates, may seem like straightforward questions with easy answers. Yet on a closer look, we can see it is anything but.

Positioning is your opportunity to set the stage for buyers, to paint the picture of why your business is special and what compelling growth opportunities exist for it going forward. Resist the urge to define your business and industry too narrowly, thus missing the opportunity to create incremental value.

> Resist the urge to define your business and industry too narrowly, thus missing the opportunity to create incremental value.

In more extreme cases, poor positioning can kill billion-dollar deals, as we'll see shortly. But exceptional positioning can help turn a ho-hum credit card company into a financial services powerhouse or allow a long-shot monopolistic merger to clear regulatory oversight hurdles and close.

## POSITIONING IN MARKETING AND PUBLIC RELATIONS

Savvy companies have been using creative and expansive positioning for decades when communicating with their shareholders to drive a higher stock price, and with their employees to attract and retain the best talent. Take, for example, Capital One, the fifth largest credit card issuer by purchase volume in the US and the country's tenth-largest bank by assets.

In their early years, before the company had gotten into the banking business and when 100 percent of their revenue came from issuing credit cards, Capital One's 1996 Annual Report made the following positioning statement. *"Despite being one of the nation's ten largest credit card issuers, we have always seen ourselves as information-based marketers rather than as a credit card company."*[10]

---

10   (Capital One Financial Corporation 1996)

*Wait, what?*

"Information-based marketing" definitely sounds sexier than "credit card company," but where did they come up with that?

To help their readers bridge the gap between what everyone outside of Capital One thought they did and what the company *wanted* them to think they did, the report added *"[Our] information-based strategy gives us the ability to customize our offerings in order to get the right product to the right customer at the right time and at the right price."*[11]

The executives at Capital One were making the point that their company was bigger than just credit cards. That at its heart, the company was focused on tracking and analyzing data from consumer responses to a variety of solicitation efforts that then was used to refine future marketing campaigns. This data-driven learning approach to marketing could support many types of businesses; credit cards happened to be what Capital One focused on at the time.

This positioning strategy worked, as Capital One has grown to over 48,000 employees, generated $28 billion of revenue in 2018, and has branched out into many financial services, including retail and commercial banking and consumer auto lending. Beyond shareholder and employee communications, though, positioning can be just as powerful in the M&A world.

---

11   Ibid.

## POSITIONING IN M&A TRANSACTIONS

How an investment bank plans to position a potential company during a sale process is so important that it is often one of the top five factors that sellers use to select which bank will represent them. But even more directly, a poor job of positioning a company can cause an M&A deal, even a multibillion-dollar M&A deal, to fail at the eleventh hour.

The Hart-Scott-Rodino (HSR) Antitrust Improvements Act of 1976 requires that potential buyers and sellers involved in large merger and acquisition transactions to notify the Federal Trade Commission (FTC) and Department of Justice (DOJ) before the deal can close. The threshold that defines "large" is updated every year based on the change in the US gross national product and currently stands at $90 million.

So, the DOJ or FTC reviews every potential M&A transaction in the US valued at over $90 million to assess whether the deal would create any antitrust concerns. If the proposed transaction is determined to harm competition or consumers, these agencies can require changes to the deal, such as spinning off assets in a particular market to a third party, or they can block them entirely. How the company and its industry are positioned plays a central role in this process.

Three types of deals need to go through the HSR process. First, routine transactions, which pose no discernible threat to competition or consumers, are quickly and unceremoniously approved, and the whole filing process is treated as a formality. These represent the vast majority, typically 96–98 percent, of HSR filings in any given year.[12] Second are those where one or both parties to the deal sees a risk that the contemplated transaction may not receive HSR approval, but the benefits to both sides of the deal are worth trying. These deals often include meaningful break-up fees that the buyer pays the seller as a consolation prize should the HSR process fail. Finally, rare exceptions exist in which the deal seems to clearly create antitrust issues and thus is widely expected to be blocked, and yet against all odds, it receives approval to proceed.

There have been many high-profile mergers that have been blocked over antitrust issues. We will look at one such example, the acquisition of US Foods by competitor Sysco, to see how positioning failed to win the day in this case. In my own investment banking career, I have had the relatively rare experience of having one of my M&A transactions flagged during the HSR review for potential antitrust issues, completely killing the deal. But what really piqued my interest in the power of positioning was neither the perfunctory approvals nor the blocked deals, but rather a high-profile example of the third category, the explicit *approval* of a deal that created a clear monopoly in a consumer-facing industry: Sirius Satellite Radio's acquisition of XM Satellite Radio in 2008.

*How were the only two satellite radio companies in the US allowed to combine?*

**The answer:** *exceptional positioning.*

---

12    (Simons and Delrahim 2018)

First, let's look at how the HSR process typically works to protect consumers and keep antitrust mergers from occurring.

## SYSCO'S ATTEMPTED ACQUISITION OF US FOODS

In December 2013, private equity firms KKR & Co. and Clayton, Dubilier & Rice agreed to sell privately held US Foods to Sysco at an enterprise value of roughly $8.2 billion, a merger that would have combined the two largest food distributors in the US. Given US Foods' position as the second-largest player in the food distribution sector, there were naturally few industry players who were sizable enough to acquire it, with the notable exception of top-ranked Sysco.

Recognizing the deal's risk of raising red flags with regulators, the M&A and legal advisors to both parties analyzed the markets in which each company operated and identified those that would likely be of highest concern. To preemptively address these concerns, US Foods arranged to sell eleven distribution centers in those problematic markets not to Sysco, but to Performance Food Group, another sizable player in the food distribution industry. With their three-way deal agreed, the parties submitted their HSR filings and waited for a response.

Despite the parties' best efforts to foresee and address likely antitrust issues, the FTC called for an injunction to the deal, concluding that the merger would lead to higher prices and diminished service for the restaurants, hotels, and schools that use food distributors. In its objection, the FTC argued that the combined company would control roughly 75 percent of the foodservice marketplace.

The injunction caused both parties to abandon the deal, and Sysco was required to pay US Foods a $300 million breakup fee, as well as a smaller $12.5 million break-up fee to Performance Food Group. This was in addition to the months of time and effort wasted in pursuing the deal, as well as the cost of advisors' fees.

*"Sysco and US Foods' decision to abandon the transaction is a victory for both competition and consumers. The evidence shows that Sysco and US Foods were strong rivals in broadline food distribution whose combination would have harmed consumers,"* Debbie Feinstein, director of the regulator's Bureau of Competition, said in a statement.[13] In other words, the FTC believed that having 75 percent of a market, food distribution in this case, controlled by a single company would be unfair to both competitors and customers. Having one company wield that much control would enable it to override normal supply/demand dynamics to artificially raise prices for customers and drive smaller competitors out of business.

*So, what went wrong?*

Ultimately, the parties failed to effectively position the companies as participating in a market larger than the specific broad-line food distribution space. Had the parties successfully positioned the companies, which had some operations outside broad-line food distribution, as participating in a much larger market, such as the US food production and

---

13   (Statement of FTC Bureau of Competition Director Debbie Feinstein on Sysco and U.S. Foods' Abandonment of Their Proposed Merger 2015)

distribution industry, their respective shares of this market would have gone down, perhaps by enough to gain approval.

* * *

Now that we have some background on how the HSR process works and how the DOJ and FTC think about whether a transaction presents antitrust issues, let's return to the curious case of satellite radio and see how exceptional positioning triumphed.

We'll see how the only two players in a specific industry used creative and expansive positioning to change the lens through which the regulators viewed the relevant competitive landscape. And in so doing, the transaction swung from being viewed as anticompetitive to one *necessary* to ensure the viability of the industry itself.

## SIRIUS SATELLITE RADIO'S ACQUISITION OF XM SATELLITE RADIO

The histories of the US's only two satellite radio companies have been intertwined from the beginning. XM was originally called American Mobile Satellite Corp. and was founded in 1988. Sirius was founded two years later and was originally called Satellite CD radio, though it dropped the reference to "CD" when it was renamed Sirius Satellite Radio in 1999. Both services spent the 1990s raising capital, obtaining broadcast licenses from the US Federal Communications Commission (FCC), investing in infrastructure, launching satellites, and securing partnerships with automakers for their receivers to be installed in new vehicles. The two services even went live within five months of each other; XM in September 2001 and Sirius in February 2002.

With over a billion dollars of capital investment needed to launch their services, both companies struggled financially during the early to mid-2000s, though each benefited from growing subscriber bases. By the time Sirius and XM announced their proposed $13 billion merger in February 2017, XM had eight million subscribers, Sirius had six million, and neither had turned an annual profit in their respective histories. After more than two decades of going head-to-head with each other, executives at both companies decided to follow the "*if you can't beat 'em, join 'em*" mantra.

Given the fact that both companies' very existence was tied to their FCC licenses, the proposed merger of the nation's only two satellite radio companies required approval from both the US Department of Justice through HSR, as well as from the FCC. After a fifty-seven-week review process, the DOJ approved the Sirius and XM merger on March 24, 2008, and on July 25, 2008, the FCC approved the merger with a 3–2 vote.

Sirius XM Radio was formed on July 29, 2008, a few days after receiving final FCC approval and seventeen months after the companies first proposed the merger. The merger brought the combined company more than eighteen million subscribers based on data at the time of the transaction. Dozens of lawmakers, consumer groups, and broadcasters had long opposed the merger, saying that the combination would create a satellite radio monopoly. But here's where exceptional positioning comes in.

The companies successfully argued that satellite radio was only one piece of the even larger market for *consumer music* and that joining forces was the only way that the two companies could survive. While this may sound like a loophole, the case was convincing. The two satellite radio providers were struggling financially, as their start-up costs had been colossal and consumers truly did have several other options. Music-enabled cellphones, iPods, music websites, and traditional radio stations all provided increased competition and were included in the relevant market in which SiriusXM operated. So rather than becoming a monopoly by combining, the companies argued that they were losing the competitive fight with all the other sources of music available to consumers. Sirius and XM argued that the merger would enable them to eliminate overlapping transmission towers and programming, both of which had been areas of heavy investment.

The positioning was indeed persuasive. The DOJ concluded that satellite radio competes with terrestrial radio, online streaming, mp3 players, and tablets, and thus saw no reason to block the deal. In the FCC's approval of the merger on a close 3–2 vote, they determined that it would not create a monopoly because of the competition on the Internet and agreed that the marketplace had changed since the two companies were originally formed, with Internet radio, iPods, and other technological advances competing for consumers. FCC chairman Kevin Martin stated, "*The merger is in the public interest and will provide consumers with greater flexibility and choices.*"[14] The two companies' positioning had indeed won the day.

---

14   (Musil 2008)

\* \* \*

We can see the power of positioning in these successful and
failed billion-dollar transactions in the HSR process. We also
learned how companies like Capital One use positioning to
reframe how its shareholders and employees perceive them.
But positioning can be just as powerful in the context of an
M&A process, and in my experience, is often underutilized.

When you and your M&A advisor create the CIM, you can
develop your own positioning statement. At its essence, it is
how you describe what your company does and how it fits
into some larger industry. And how you position your company is totally up to you. Buyers may have a hard time believing your positioning if you've strayed too far from reality, but
more often than not, your self-described positioning helps
open new possibilities in how buyers think about the future
opportunities for your business. And the more opportunities
that a buyer sees for your business to grow, the more valuable
it will be to them. That's the real power of positioning. If done
well, it moves companies from limited growth potential to
expanded possibilities.

> That's the real power of positioning.
> If done well, it moves companies
> from limited growth potential to
> expanded possibilities.

This is exactly what Capital One was doing. It didn't want
to be confined by the public markets and its employee base

to only participating in the credit card industry, which was finite albeit large. In describing themselves as "information-based marketers," they placed themselves in a virtually infinite market. They started applying their marketing strategy to issuing credit cards and then expanded into other financial services. They even tested unrelated lines of business, like flowers and cell phones. Who knows what markets they will be serving in the next ten years? We only know they'll be using data-driven marketing analytics to be successful.

We saw the same dynamic at work in the Sirius XM merger. Positioning expanded the relevant market to include all manner of consumer music delivery options, diluting the concern around how large the combined satellite radio audiences would be. Further, the parties argued successfully that if the merger were blocked and one or both satellite radio providers collapsed under the weight of their operating losses, consumers would be worse off for not having any satellite radio option at all.

In the next chapter, we will learn about the various types of buyers that you should consider when starting an M&A process and the process by which you can evaluate which ones might be right for you to approach.

**ACTION ITEM**
- *Think creatively and expansively about your company.* Rather than describe exactly what your company does today at ground level, pull back and view it from cruising altitude. Think about what value you provide

to customers and what related types of products or services they also value. Think too about what new types of customers might also value your current offering. Then try to capture all of that in your positioning. Not only will it help drive increased value for your business with the most likely buyers, but it will also increase the likelihood that your company will attract the attention of more tangential buyers and add competitive pressure to your M&A process.

# CHAPTER 8

# UNDERSTAND YOUR OPTIONS

———

Business owners often have a strong sense of who they believe will be the ultimate buyer of their company, and in my twenty-plus years of experience, they are almost always wrong.

Frankly, investment bankers are not any better at predicting the ultimate buyer. Too many variables are at play to know with any degree of certainty which potential buyers will prevail in a particular sale process. While a seller's misplaced confidence in a given buyer may seem inconsequential to the overall outcome, often the perception that one company is the most likely buyer drives poor decisions that can jeopardize the entire sale process.

It is critically important for business owners to fully understand the various options available to them, both in terms of buyer categories and specific companies within each. Depending on the seller's desired outcome, their options may include domestic and international strategic (corporate) buyers, private equity, and other types of financial buyers, or both. It also may include groups that will take a minority stake in your business, in addition to those groups who look to acquire controlling majority positions in companies.

It is only with a full understanding of the available options that sellers can make informed decisions about which buyers to contact in the first place, and ultimately, with which buyer they choose to transact. Otherwise, they risk looking back on the sale of their business with regret at stones left unturned.

Let's look at a case where preconceived opinions about specific buyers nearly cratered a sale process.

\* \* \*

Gavin Price, an investment banking colleague of mine, recently recounted a story about a healthcare services business that he worked on selling a few years ago. The client, Keisha Lancaster, had strong preconceived ideas about who would be the best buyer for her business, and the process that unfolded clearly illustrated the importance of the seller's keeping an open mind.

"*Right from our first meeting with Keisha, while we were still competing for the engagement with several other investment banks, we could see that she felt very strongly about certain industry buyers.*" In that pitch meeting, Gavin presented his firm's qualifications to run an M&A auction process for Keisha's business, including how he would position the company to buyers, how each phase of the process would unfold, and a representative sample of the types of buyers they would recommend contacting.

As Gavin began the section of his presentation on potential buyers, Keisha interrupted with observations on two of the companies that Gavin's firm had profiled. First, she assured Gavin that she knew that Latham Corp. would be the ultimate buyer of her business. Latham had been calling on her over the past several years, expressing a strong interest in acquiring her business whenever she decided to sell. They were well-regarded in the industry, had made several successful acquisitions, and had been aggressively pursuing Keisha for a long time.

Keisha was also sure that she did not want to contact Royal Industries, another market participant Gavin profiled as a representative potential buyer. Keisha believed that Royal had a poor reputation in the industry, didn't see a compelling rationale for combining her business with theirs, and was not aware of any acquisitions that Royal had made.

In Keisha's mind, the M&A process should focus entirely on Latham, and she was indifferent about whether any additional buyers were contacted, with the singular exception of Royal, who she wanted to strike completely from the process.

Gavin took note of Keisha's feedback and continued his presentation.

Shortly after engaging Gavin's firm to sell her business, Keisha introduced Gavin to Samuel Waters, her contact at Latham, who was excited to learn that Keisha had decided to sell her company, but also somewhat discouraged that Gavin's firm had been engaged to run a process. *"Given the relationship that we've built over the years,"* Samuel told Keisha, *"we expected that you'd give us the first look, not hire a banker and market the business to other buyers. We don't like to play in auctions."* Samuel asked that Keisha give Latham a sixty-day exclusive period to come to an agreement on deal terms without contacting any other buyers. Following Gavin's advice, Keisha declined to go exclusive with Latham but encouraged them to work with Gavin through the process, which Samuel reluctantly agreed to do.

As Keisha reviewed the full list of potential buyers that Gavin's firm presented for her approval, she again stopped on Royal. *"I don't think we should contact them at all,"* Keisha commented, *"I can't believe we'd ever want to sell to them."* Based on Gavin's research, he highlighted the strategic fit that he believed existed with Royal and encouraged Keisha to reconsider. Ultimately, she acquiesced and allowed Royal to be included in the potential buyer calls.

Gavin's firm finalized the Confidential Information Memorandum and began contacting those groups on the approved buyer list. After interested parties signed a Confidentiality Agreement and received the CIM, they submitted first-round bids, which would then be used to select bidders to have face-to-face meetings with management. Sure enough, Latham was the highest of the fifteen initial bids received, with Royal solidly in the middle of the pack. Keisha again raised the idea of setting aside the other buyers in favor of moving forward exclusively with Latham, but Gavin pushed back, recommending against committing to one buyer prior to even having a single in-depth meeting with them. Ultimately, Keisha agreed to have management meetings with the top eight groups, including Latham and Royal.

On the eve of the first meeting, Keisha received some bad news. Her largest customer, which accounted for about 30 percent of sales, was temporarily halting its purchases from Keisha due to weakening demand in its business. Suddenly, Keisha's growth targets for the current year needed to be revised downward, which she communicated to each of the eight buyers during the in-person meetings. While the groups remain interested, the reduction in sales dampened the excitement level among the buyers, and they indicated that their first-round bids would likely need to be revised downward accordingly.

In addition, Keisha was surprised when her meeting with the favored Latham didn't go as well as many of the others. Samuel and his colleagues didn't seem to have a strong understanding of Keisha's lines of business, and they lacked the enthusiasm that had existed during their informal discussions over the years.

After the meeting with Latham ended, Keisha shared with Gavin her concern that Latham may be losing interest and how glad she was that there were other competing bidders. Keisha also noticed that the meeting with Royal went much better than she'd expected and considered that perhaps her belief in their poor reputation was unwarranted, as she enjoyed meeting the Royal executives that attended the meeting.

When the deadline for final bids arrived, Gavin received offers from five of the eight groups that had visited with Keisha and her management team. Royal, the black sheep, was the top bidder, and Latham had dropped out without submitting any offer at all, citing concerns over the slowdown at Keisha's top customer and there being less of a strategic fit with their core business than they had originally believed there would be.

*"We selected Royal as the winning buyer,"* Gavin recalls, *"and it turns out they were the most accommodating buyer we could have hoped for."* Royal sailed through their confirmatory due diligence without raising any issues, and the negotiations of the legal documentation, the Purchase & Sale Agreement, also went smoothly. The sale of Keisha's business to Royal was completed ahead of schedule and at a purchase price that exceeded her initial expectations.

*"I'm so glad I followed Gavin's advice to include Royal in the process and not focus too heavily on Latham,"* Keisha noted. *"Otherwise, we would have been left at the altar when Latham backed out, and we would have had to restart the process from the beginning, wasting valuable months in the setback."*

## AVOID PREJUDGING POTENTIAL BUYERS

It is natural for business owners to have preconceived ideas about other companies in their industry. It would be unusual if they didn't.

Most owners thrive on market intel and like to keep track of competitors' successes and missteps in the market. It is a good business practice to keep an eye on direct and indirect competitors, and in doing so over a long period, it is natural that opinions about them are formed. The former employees of these companies are interviewed and perhaps hired. Conversations take place on the floor on industry trade shows or in the airport afterward. All this information can be useful in a company's strategic planning process, but is largely useless in informing an M&A process.

The reason for this is simple. Until a potential buyer is presented with an M&A opportunity, neither you nor they really know for sure how they'll react.

> Until a potential buyer is presented with an M&A opportunity, neither you nor they really know for sure how they'll react.

Maybe they've been trying to butter you up for years by expressing overt interest in acquiring your business, as was the case with Keisha and Latham Corp., in the hopes of getting a preemptive look at your business without competition from other buyers. That's a great strategy from the buyer's perspective; little cost in terms of time and effort for a potentially lucrative chance to buy your business at a below-market value.

We all know that strategic plans are fluid and must adapt to changing market conditions. This dynamic affects strategic buyers' M&A interests all the time. Perhaps making an acquisition of a company just like yours was at the top of the Board's list of strategic priorities last year. Then markets changed, internal issues arose, or strategic focus shifted. This year, they are seeking acquisitions in different market sectors. Of course, the same changes can work in reverse, bringing a previously uninterested buyer into play as they react to changing market conditions.

Investment bankers will look at a company's acquisition history to ascertain how likely that buyer would be to acquire their client's business. While this is certainly helpful data, it is by no means definitive. I've seen strategic buyers who have made a series of acquisitions exactly like the company I was selling express no interest in my client, citing their need to integrate previous deals before making new ones. Or they said they were done buying businesses in that market segment and had moved on to other niches. Other buyers with the same historical acquisition profile have been hyper-aggressive in bidding for my client, seeking to build critical mass within the niche. You never know what forces are at work, what strategic decisions are being made, within the Boardrooms and executive suites of potential buyers. That is until you approach them and give them a real, live opportunity to consider.

With this understanding, one benefit of running a competitive M&A process becomes clear. If you can't know with much confidence which buyer will be most aggressive in bidding for your company, you should contact multiple buyers at one time. That way, when some buyers surprisingly flake out, others surprisingly step forward. You can't know with 100 percent certainty that you'd never sell to a particular potential buyer under any circumstance and at any price. I would counsel you to include as many buyers on the list as possible and let the process sort the wheat from the chaff.

## UNDERSTAND YOUR OPTIONS

Sometimes my clients equate exiting their business with "selling out" to their primary competitor, and in most situations, this is not a pleasant thought. This aversion to turning their enterprise over to a despised competitor, including the feelings of the disloyalty to employees it would create, leads many business owners to turn their back on the whole M&A process. If you have certain competitors or other companies that you would never want to acquire your business, no worries—you don't have to include them in the process at all.

> If you have certain competitors or other companies that you would never want to acquire your business, no worries— you don't have to include them in the process at all.

The truth of the matter is different; there are many types of buyers from which to choose, each with their own unique characteristics.

M&A professionals often talk about two types of buyers: strategic and financial, yet there are subcategories of each that are meaningful to understand as you think about what the ideal buyer for your business might look like.

## STRATEGIC BUYERS

Corporate acquirers, whether they operate in competitive or complementary lines of business, are termed *strategic buyers*, because their acquisitions are focused on targets that provide a strategic fit with their overall growth strategy. Strategic buyers always have a *"Make versus Buy"* decision. Would it be quicker and/or more cost-effective to acquire a given business or to invest in creating the same capabilities from scratch in-house?

Strategic buyers can offer many attractive advantages to a seller. Chief among them is the ability for the selling owner to retire from the business after a short transition period, typically three to six months. In addition, for business owners that desire a full exit through a sale of 100 percent of their ownership, strategic buyers are likely the best alternative.

The benefits to your business of selling to a strategic buyer can also be attractive. Access to the buyer's larger base of customers, more robust sales team, broader distribution capabilities, or a better sourcing network can all have a significant positive impact on your business's future. The primary downsides to strategic buyers are the potential loss of the business's independent identity and the possibility of cost-cutting, such as elimination of back-office functions that can be handled by the buyer's current staff.

Strategic buyers can be further categorized by the location of their corporate headquarters. *International strategic buyers* often operate their US divisions independently with a hands-off approach, particularly if they don't already have substantial operating businesses in the US. *Domestic strategic buyers*, on the other hand, are more likely to have higher levels of integration with their acquisition targets, yielding more efficient operations and cost savings that drive higher earnings to the bottom line.

## FINANCIAL BUYERS

*Financial buyers* are professional investors that acquire private companies with the goal of improving them before selling them several years later to realize a return on their investment. Hundreds of financial buyers are looking for small to medium-sized private businesses to acquire in the US, generally falling into one of three categories:

1. Private Equity Groups
2. Fundless Sponsors
3. Family Offices

*Private equity groups* are by far the largest cadre of financial buyers, both in terms of quantity and purchasing power. According to PitchBook, 563 new middle-market PE funds (funds of less than a billion dollars) were raised in the 2016–2018 timeframe, representing an aggregate of $148 billion of capital to invest in private companies.[15]

The private equity model is simple and straightforward. A PE firm (the general partner, or GP) raises a pool of capital from investors (limited partners, or LPs) to then make equity investments in private companies. Private equity LPs often comprise insurance companies, pension funds, and college

---

15   (PitchBook Data, Inc. 2019)

endowments that allocate a portion of their capital to private equity and other alternative investments, which offer higher returns with higher levels of risk.

Once a private equity fund raises the targeted amount of capital, the fund is closed to new LPs and the clock begins. PE funds typically have to invest all the committed capital in acquired businesses, called portfolio companies, within the first three to five years and then exit all the investments and fully return the capital to their investors within ten years. GPs earn an annual management fee, often 2 percent, of the total fund amount and then take a meaningful portion, often 20 percent, of the gains the fund generates. To increase the potential return on invested capital, PE firms will acquire businesses using a combination of their fund's capital and bank debt that will be repaid by the portfolio company over time.

> To increase the potential return on invested capital, PE firms will acquire businesses using a combination of their fund's capital and bank debt that will be repaid by the portfolio company over time.

Because PE firms are professional investors and not business operators, they will control the Board of Directors, but rely completely on the existing management teams to run their portfolio companies. As a result, PE firms will motivate their management teams to increase the value of the business through options and the ability to own a minority portion of equity. The quality of management and their desire to remain in leadership positions are so important to most PE firms that they will not pursue acquisitions where management is not strong or wants to retire post-closing.

> The quality of management and their desire to remain in leadership positions are so important to most PE firms that they will not pursue acquisitions where management is not strong or wants to retire post-closing.

*Fundless Sponsors* are groups that pursue the same investment strategy as PE firms, but have not raised a fund of committed capital. Instead, they maintain a network of potential backers and raise the capital needed to make an acquisition on a deal-by-deal basis. For this reason, fundless sponsors are viewed as having more risk of a deal falling apart before closing than PE firms that control a fund of committed capital. That said, I have worked with a number of very successful fundless sponsors who were great partners to their portfolio companies.

*Family offices* make investments in private businesses like a private equity group, but their capital comes from one or more high-net-worth individuals or families. As such, they are considered more *patient capital* since they don't have time pressure to sell their investments and return capital to LPs. In fact, many family offices take a long-term approach to their portfolio companies or may even plan to hold their businesses indefinitely. Family offices also typically use less bank debt in their acquisitions, which many business owners find more comforting.

### PE-BACKED STRATEGIC BUYERS

Once a private equity firm has made an investment in a stand-alone business, or platform company, they often seek to grow that platform by making smaller, add-on acquisitions. This *PE-backed platform company* thus becomes a hybrid category of buyer, blending the characteristics of both a strategic and financial buyer. It is common for platform companies to be particularly aggressive in pursuing add-on acquisitions in the first twelve to twenty-four months of PE ownership, when sufficient time exists to reap the rewards of the add-on growth strategy before the PE firm needs to sell the overall platform.

> It is common for platform companies to be particularly aggressive in pursuing add-on acquisitions in the first twelve to twenty-four months of PE ownership, when sufficient time exists to reap the rewards of the add-on growth strategy before the PE firm needs to sell the overall platform.

\* \* \*

When you have a full understanding of the range of strategic and financial buyers that exist and what each can bring to the table in a potential transaction, you can make the best choice of partner for you and your business. For some sellers, a strategic buyer offers the ideal option for a successful exit. For others with a longer-term horizon and appetite to continue leading their company forward, private equity is the perfect partner.

Entrepreneur and self-made millionaire Roger Booth knows quite a bit about the power of partnering with private equity groups. He sold his industrial services company, Rosemont Enterprises, to three different PE firms over the course of a twelve-year period. Founded by Booth in 2001, Rosemont has grown to become one of the largest providers of commercial equipment and facility maintenance services in the country with over $700 million in revenue and 1,700 employees. But Rosemont would not be a tenth of what it is today if Roger hadn't first sold a stake in the business to a private equity firm fifteen years ago.

\* \* \*

Rosemont experienced tremendous growth in its first four years of existence and, by 2005, was generating over $20 million in annual revenue. Drawing on his previous experience working for Fortune 100 companies, Roger had been careful to invest in the foundational aspects of the business that would underpin long-term growth, a key step many entrepreneurs overlook. *"We had a pretty professional business for its size at the time,"* Roger remembers. *"We had a formal strategic plan, a strong IT system, and pretty good operational data. We had a clearly articulated value proposition and core values, as well as written goals and objectives, an annual employee review process, and an active training program.*" With a solid foundation in place and plenty of opportunities for growth ahead, Roger could see that the business that he had created had the potential to be $100 million or more in revenue.

Owning a business growing as fast as Rosemont presented drawbacks for Roger on the personal front. Most notably, he had taken little cash out of the business, choosing instead to reinvest it back into the business to support Rosemont's rapid growth. With a growing family at home and a desire to ensure college and retirement funds were in place, Roger considered diversifying his net worth, which was almost entirely tied up in the business, by selling all or a portion of the company and investing the proceeds in more traditional financial assets.

"*One of the key success factors I saw in selling a business is getting the timing right,*" notes Roger. Business owners are understandably reluctant to sell their companies during periods of growth, afraid to miss out on the benefits of its future expansion. Yet when businesses have peaked and are stagnate or on the decline, buyers are no longer interested at attractive valuations. Most buyers don't want to "catch a falling knife" by acquiring a company that has plateaued or is in decline and will thus bid very low or even not at all.

> Most buyers don't want to "catch a falling knife" by acquiring a company that has plateaued or is in decline and will thus bid very low or even not at all.

For Roger, selling some, but not all, of his company to a private equity firm while Rosemont was still growing seemed to make the most sense. Given the company's impressive growth trajectory and strong internal infrastructure, he hoped Rosemont would attract a deep field of interested PE firms eager to invest in the business. *"The plan to sell a portion of the equity in Rosemont would enable me to 'take some chips off the table,' to use the old poker adage, while continuing to have long-term upside potential through the equity in the company that I would retain post-closing."* This strategy would address both Roger's desire for personal liquidity and position the company on a faster path to growth going forward.

Roger engaged a local investment banking firm to run an M&A process focused on private equity firms. As suspected, Rosemont received significant interest from the market, with over fifty PE buyers submitting first-round bids. Roger and his investment bankers invited the highest eleven bidders to visit the company for in-person presentations on the business. He and his top executives met with each potential buyer during roughly three-hour meetings and shared their vision for Rosemont, while also interviewing each buyer on topics ranging from their past investment track record to their style of working with the management teams of the companies they bought.

One group, a $300 million PE fund called Queensgate Capital from Connecticut, stood out from the rest. *"I really connected with Queensgate's founder, Diane Newsome,"* Roger recalls. *"She had a successful track record of working with CEOs to drive faster growth than they had previously achieved on their own, and her management style and high degree of candor really resonated with me."* Though Roger also liked several of the other potential buyers that he met with, Queensgate quickly became the front-runner in Roger's mind.

One way that Diane had helped other Queensgate portfolio companies grow was by encouraging their CEOs to set strategic milestones and then serving as an accountability partner to ensure the CEO was executing against that plan. Roger recalls, *"I remember Diane saying that even she personally used accountability partners to push herself to grow Queensgate, so she understood the power of feeling responsible to someone else to push harder than one would otherwise if left to themselves."*

Roger selected Queensgate as the winning bidder and closed the transaction a few months later. While many business owners may have been content to maintain a $20 million in revenue business, Roger was still hungry to expand, and he found Queensgate's focus on growth contagious. *"Learning more and more about Queensgate's prior success stories, of doubling or tripling their investments through growth, was inspirational for my team and me and, at the same time, sparked a sense of competition,"* Roger noted. *"If those other companies could do it, why couldn't we?"* This new source of inspiration resonated throughout Rosemont's management team, as they felt that, with Queensgate as their partner, growth that had seemed out of reach previously now seemed attainable.

During Queensgate's tenure with Rosemont, the company doubled revenue to approximately $50 million from 2005 to 2012, a fact made particularly remarkable considering it also spanned the 2008–2009 recession. When the company had rebounded from the recession and resumed pre-crisis growth trends, Roger and Queensgate agreed it was time to sell the business a second time, providing full liquidity for Queensgate and partial liquidity for Roger and the other management shareholders.

In 2012, Rosemont engaged a larger investment bank than it had used before to market the business, which resulted in the sale of Rosemont to MacTavish Partners, an $800-million private equity group with an aggressive appetite for growth through acquisitions. Within six months, MacTavish Partners enabled Rosemont to make a large acquisition in an adjacent market segment, nearly doubling Rosemont's size and bringing significant cross-selling opportunities into the two businesses' respective customer bases.

Over the subsequent five years, Roger and Rosemont's team, with the backing of MacTavish, made twenty-three add-on acquisitions. Those companies, along with significant organic growth in the base business, propelled Rosemont to over $700 million in revenue in just five years, when the business was marketed by an investment bank for the third time and sold to an even larger $1.5 billion private equity fund.

In late 2018, Roger hired a full-time CEO and currently serves as Chairman of the Board, while Rosemont continues to grow larger every year. Looking back on his company's eighteen-year journey from being a founder-owned start-up to generating over $700 million of revenue with its third private equity partner, Roger is clear on one thing. *"I always viewed each sale to the next private equity group not as the end of the line for my ownership in the company, but as a significant step forward for both myself and Rosemont,"* Roger observes. *"I am 100 percent certain that the tremendous growth that Rosemont has achieved since 2012 would not have been possible without my three private equity partners."* Having professional investors as partners was the secret weapon that Roger needed to create a business *seven times larger* than the $100-million goal he thought Rosemont could one day reach.

## HOW TO ATTRACT PE BUYERS

I have found that financial buyers, like the three private equity firms that helped Roger build a nationwide industrial services business with $700 million in revenue, are often either completely unknown to middle-market business owners or severely misunderstood. Most founders are unfamiliar with what financial buyers are, how they operate, or what benefits they offer. If a company owner has heard of private equity, they often have a vaguely negative impression of them, but are unsure exactly why.

To be clear, private equity groups and other financial buyers are not the right partners for all businesses. Companies that have not reached roughly $2 million in earnings will be too small to attract much PE interest. Some industries, such as those that are highly cyclical, seasonal, or asset-heavy, may also be viewed as unattractive to financial buyers because companies that operated within them do not have the reliably consistent cash flows needed to repay debt. And some companies may not operate in large enough markets to be as scalable as financial buyers typically require.

The most powerful inhibitor of PE interest in middle-market businesses, however, is the absence of a motivated management team that will invest alongside the new financial buyer and lead the business forward to new heights. Roger saw his first sale to Queensgate Capital as not the final lap of the race, but merely a pitstop for fresh tires and more fuel. He still had the drive and desire to lead the business forward and saw the growth potential that a powerful financial partner would help him realize.

To be attractive to financial buyers, one of two situations must exist. Either the company's current owners are still in their prime, want to reinvest a portion of their proceeds in the business alongside the new PE buyer, and see this event as the next step in a longer growth journey. Or, if the current owners want to retire, a second-level management team must be in place to lead the company forward. If neither of these conditions exists, the business may indeed still be salable, but only to strategic buyers who can fold the company into their existing organizational structure.

* * *

First-time sellers often believe that their only option to exit is to sell their business to a direct competitor, which can be a tough pill to swallow. In reality, many other options exist, each of which offers unique benefits for both the seller and the future of the business being sold. Only by fully understanding your options and not myopically focusing on one buyer to the exclusion of others can you ensure a successful, regret-free exit.

In the next chapter, we'll look ahead in the M&A process and learn that there are many variables to consider when selecting from competing buyers for your business. Often, maximizing price is not the only objective, and the best buyer for your business may not be the highest bidder.

## ACTION ITEMS

- *Start with an open mind.* As you think about a future buyer for your business, take a fresh perspective and consider a wide variety of buyers, including strategic and financial buyers. Consider not only direct competitors but also tangential strategic buyers that may view your company as complementary or as a means to enter new markets or customer segments.

- *Consider your appetite for continued leadership.* Are you viewing an exit as a well-deserved means to fully retire and enjoy the financial rewards from having successfully built a business? Or would you like to continue to lead the business through its next phase of growth, but with additional capital for growth or personal net worth diversification? If you are planning to transition out of the business in the near term, are there successors in place that can step into your leadership shoes? No right or wrong answers exist for these and other related questions, but listen to your responses and let them shape which types of buyers to contact during your sale process.

PART 3

# WINNING THE M&A PROCESS

## CHAPTER 9

# FOCUS ON MORE THAN PRICE

———

Ask any business owner what the primary goal of a sale process is, and chances are their top answer will be to maximize purchase price. And that's understandable; a big payday is clearly one of the top reasons why owners sell their business and probably why you bought this book. But price is not the only factor you should consider when evaluating exit alternatives. In fact, I have seen several transactions where top dollar did not win the day. Savvy sellers recognize there is more to maximize in an exit transaction than purchase price alone.

\* \* \*

The time had come to make a final decision that would impact the lives of hundreds of employees and set the future course for the IT consulting firm that Velocity's managing partners had so painstakingly built over the past eighteen years.

As the five owners gathered around the conference room table, their investment bankers passed out a summary of the final offers, though no one needed the handout for reference. The partners had arrived at this moment after months of work in the M&A process and had been wrestling with the decision now before them ever since the Letters of Intent were received four days ago.

*"As you know, we have three offers on the table,"* their M&A advisor began, *"a strategic buyer at $110 million, a family office at $108 million, and a second family office at $104 million. We've worked each of the bids as much as possible, and we don't think there is any more room for them to move. Shall we notify the strategic buyer that they won?"*

The partners eyed each other around the table, and with knowing nods, reconfirmed the decision they'd reached the night before.

*"Actually, we've decided to pick the third-place finisher, the family office at $104 million,"* the lead partner said. Though they would forgo $6 million of incremental purchase price, roughly a million dollars after taxes to each of them, the partners were 100 percent certain this was the right decision.

Why would sellers forego two higher offers for a seemingly inferior one? As it turns out, finding the best long-term partner for the future of their business and its employees was more important to them than extracting the last dollar of the purchase price from the market.

* * *

Velocity Ventures is a national management consulting firm that helps bridge the gap between business and technology headquartered in Arlington, Virginia. Velocity delivers transformation, customer engagement, data and analytics, and custom IT solutions for private businesses, public companies, and government agencies. The firm's collaborative approach helps organizations grow their business, engage with customers, and turn information into powerful data assets.

Velocity experienced significant growth over its first two decades, landing on the Inc. 5000 list of the nation's fastest-growing companies several years in a row. Though the firm had grown to over 550 employees and four locations from Atlanta, Georgia to Baltimore, Maryland, Velocity remained independent and privately owned by its five senior partners, each of whom has been with the company for nearly twenty years and holds an executive-level position at the firm.

As the firm grew in size and reputation, potential buyers took note. In the early 2000s, Velocity's partners were approached by a private equity firm interested in acquiring a majority position in the firm, and several years later, another PE firm made an offer for the business. In both cases, the partners were intrigued by the standard PE proposition: sell a majority of the business to achieve a multimillion-dollar payout, while continuing to operate the firm and participate in the next phase of growth through the portion of their equity that they didn't sell.

As they got into deeper discussions with each of these groups, however, they reached the same conclusion in both cases. While the valuations these buyers presented were attractive, private equity was not the right partner for Velocity at that point in the firm's life cycle. The senior partners just could not get comfortable with the idea that the firm would be taking on tens of millions of dollars of debt as part of a PE acquisition. *"We had always operated with little to no debt, which enabled us to be more flexible and weather the economic and business cycles in our industry,"* one partner recalled. *"The leverage those PE firms planned to use to acquire our company would have left us burdened by debt service payments that might drag us under during periods of economic softness."* The partners were unwilling to risk their company's survival to receive a lucrative payday by selling to a private equity firm.

In addition to the debt, the partners bristled at two other aspects of selling to a private equity group. First, PE firms need to increase the value of the businesses they acquire over a three- to five-year period and then sell them to the next buyer so they can return the gains to their investors. The Velocity partners had concerns that it would be hard to retain key employees if they knew that another sale would be looming in the not-too-distant future. They feared employees would view the PE firm as a temporary owner too short-sighted to make investments to support long-term growth initiatives. Further, selling to a PE firm today meant that the decision about when to sell the company again, and to whom, would be out of the partners' hands. The idea that Velocity might one day be sold to a strategic buyer that would lay off staff or take other drastic measures to generate incremental returns might be enough to make valuable employees seek more stable employment at other firms in the industry.

The partners also began to see trust issues emerge during the discussions with both firms. As one example, the agreed-upon composition of the Board of Directors changed from a five-person Board, with three members from the PE firm and two management members, to a nine-person Board, with six members from the PE firm and only three management seats, minimizing the influence of the management team in favor of the PE shop. This type of trust-breaking before the deal was even closed did not bode well for an ongoing relationship, and so the Velocity partners in each case walked away from lucrative exits rather than risk selling their company to someone they didn't trust.

After that, the partners decided to eschew unsolicited interest from potential PE partners and continued to focus on growing the business and its base of talented employees.

By 2014, though, Velocity's co-founders decided it was time to look for a buyer for the firm to enable them to retire, and they engaged an investment banking firm to help them evaluate strategic alternatives. The M&A advisors laid out three primary types of buyers for consideration: strategic buyers, private equity groups, and family offices. While valuations from PE buyers in the IT consulting space were high, the partners concluded based on their prior experiences with the two PE buyers to exclude that buyer category from the process. "We just knew that private equity was not a good fit for Velocity's business model and culture," remarked one of Velocity's partners.

The partners were interested in the potential merits of selling to a strategic buyer, which would bring new client relationships and access to complementary services that would accelerate Velocity's growth. The partners warned their bankers, however, that culture fit with strategic buyers would be critical, as they knew the damage on morale and employee retention that could result from a culture mismatch. Velocity's partners understood how the unique culture that they had painstakingly cultivated in their firm was one of the top reasons they had that could attract and maintain such a talented and dedicated workforce. They couldn't afford to choose the wrong strategic buyer that would disrupt that culture and put the firm's future success in jeopardy.

As they considered the potential buyer landscape, Velocity's owners were also intrigued by the prospect of selling to a family office, which seemed to offer attractive characteristics of both a strategic and PE buyer. As we discussed in the previous chapter, family offices are similar to private equity firms in that both are financial buyers that invest in businesses and allow them to remain independent. Yet unlike PE firms, family offices are investing their own capital, and, therefore, do not need to sell their portfolio companies in a subsequent transaction within a fixed period. In fact, many family offices are content to own their portfolio companies forever; Warren Buffett's Berkshire Hathaway is probably the most well-known example of this type of buyer.

With this direction, Velocity's investment bankers ran an M&A process focused on strategic acquirers and family offices and received attractive initial interest from both types of buyers. By the time final offers were due, the field of buyers had been narrowed to three, an international strategic buyer with the highest offer and two-family offices in second and third place.

In the weeks leading up to the offer deadline, the partners had wisely spent time with the leadership teams of each of the three potential suitors to gain as much insight as they could on the intangibles they believed should also be weighed in their decision, in addition to price. The partners believed that this information, such as how involved each buyer would be in managing Velocity post-closing, how the management team of previous acquisitions felt about each buyer, and the overall vision that each suitor had for Velocity's future, would be critically important in how the deal would be received by Velocity's employees, and by extension, the ultimate success of the transaction.

*"When we envisioned announcing the deal to our employees, we wanted to be sincerely proud of who we picked to buy our firm and why we chose them,"* recalled one partner. *"We wanted to be able to look each and every employee in the eye and tell them that this decision would benefit Velocity as a firm and each of them individually."*

The partners learned valuable insights from spending time with the final buyers. For example, the international strategic buyer was viewed in their home markets as a third-tier, low-cost IT staffing firm and was planning to use the acquisition of Velocity, a high-end IT consulting firm, to bridge to a higher-level client.

One of the family offices was in the midst of a leadership succession from the patriarch, who had built the family's wealth through a successful career in the automotive industry, to his son, who was fresh out of business school and eager to make a mark on the portfolio companies with his new MBA. It was clear to Velocity that the inexperienced, yet eager, son would be calling the shots if that buyer prevailed.

The other family office, however, was different. Grayhill Capital is the investing arm of a specialty insurance provider and makes strategic investments in businesses that operate outside of the specialty insurance marketplace. Grayhill Capital is pursuing a strategy similar to that of Berkshire Hathaway: use profits from the insurance business to make controlling investments in straightforward, well-performing operating companies and hold them as investments indefinitely.

As one of Velocity's partners recalls, *"Grayhill told us they wouldn't be the highest bidder, but their offer would be fair and easy to understand. They assured us they would never sell one of their portfolio companies, and that their involvement in each of their portfolio companies was limited to three aspects: understand what they do, help remove roadblocks, and open up new avenues for growth."* Velocity's owners loved the fact that their employees would take comfort that the business would not be sold again, a major drawback from their earlier dealings with PE firms. And Grayhill's hands-off approach, which focuses on facilitating growth and empowering the existing management team to continue leading the company, sounded much better than being micromanaged by the heir to an automotive fortune.

Sure enough, when the final offers came in, Grayhill wasn't the high bidder, but they were by far the preferred choice.

In a perfect example of how price should never be the sole determinant when choosing a buyer, Velocity found in Grayhill an ideal buyer that they were proud to introduce to their employees.

Velocity's co-founders summed it up well. *"At Velocity, our people are our business, and they are passionate about what they do. Our culture provides the opportunity for them to express their ideas and use their talents to create unique solutions with our customers."* Another senior partner added, *"When looking for a partner, we knew that we needed to find one that could understand Velocity's culture going forward, and we are excited to have Grayhill as that partner."* By investing the time to really get to know each of the finalist bidders and realizing that price wasn't the most important factor when selecting the next owner of their business, Velocity's senior partners found an ideal partner in Grayhill Capital that they would have missed if they'd defaulted to the top bidder.

\* \* \*

As we see in Velocity's sale to Grayhill, many important factors beyond price should be optimized when choosing the ultimate buyer of your business. Entity-to-entity criteria, such as the degree of cultural fit, reputation compatibility, and alignment of strategic vision, between the buying and selling companies are critical to a successful M&A outcome. Likewise, person-to-person fit, such as management styles and personality compatibility of the executives from both the buyer and seller, can make the difference between success and failure in a newly combined entity.

> Likewise, person-to-person fit, such as management styles and personality compatibility of the executives from both the buyer and seller, can make the difference between success and failure in a newly combined entity.

## A FOUR-STEP PROCESS TO FIND THE BEST BUYER FOR YOUR BUSINESS

To truly maximize the overall exit process and create the most successful M&A outcome possible, I recommend that my clients use the following four-step process to narrow the field of potential buyers from a broad pool of options to the best buyer for their particular business.

1. **Use Qualitative Factors to Pick Categories of Buyers**—As we learned in Chapter 8, many types of potential purchasers exist, broadly grouped into Strategic and Financial buyers, and further refined to categories such as international strategic or family office. When deciding which types of buyers to include in your M&A process, consider such qualitative factors such as how they will approach your desired role with the company post-closing and whether particular types of buyers can create new growth opportunities for your business. To keep your options open, only eliminate those categories of buyers that have a fatal mismatch. If you wouldn't sell to one type of buyer, or even a specific company, at any price, then it makes no sense to include them in your M&A process.

2. **Use Price to Weed Out the Tire Kickers**—After contacting the universe of acceptable potential buyers and sharing your Confidential Information Memorandum with those interested in learning more about your company, price is a great tool to eliminate discount buyers and focus only on those groups with the highest range of value. Comparing the initial indications of interest that each interested purchaser submits will allow you to see where the market sees the overall value of your business. From this array of buyers and associated valuation ranges, you'll invite those buyers offering the most attractive prices to continue in the process to the management presentation phase, while kindly dismissing the rest of the field.

3. **Use Qualitative Factors to Narrow the Field of Finalists**—Once you've used price to select the set of buyers that you would like to meet with, set price aside again. Having passed the first cut of the initial indication of interest phase, the buyers still left in the process will have each offered an acceptable valuation range. Refrain from sharing each visitor's preliminary valuation range with the executive team members that will participate in the meetings with potential buyers. Rather than have them biased for or against a given purchaser based on price, going into the buyer visits blind to price allows the team to gauge those qualitative factors, such as alignment of strategic direction and personality styles, that are crucial to a successful outcome. Many of my clients even develop an internal rating rubric and score each group at the conclusion of their meeting to provide consistent feedback across the field.

4. **Use Price Again to Get Best Outcome**—Using the results from the previous round, divide the field into two groups: acceptable and unacceptable buyers. Disregarding those buyers deemed unacceptable due to lack of fit and focusing only on those groups where an acceptable level of fit exists, you can once again bring valuation back into the equation. Use the power of the competitive process among this group of finalists to negotiate the best price and terms possible, knowing that you'll be happy with whichever of the finalists steps up and outbids the rest of the field.

This method is designed to yield the best outcome of both strategic fit and top price, starting with a broad array of options and creating the optimum outcome as a final result. If we look back at Velocity's sale, they followed this approach step by step. In Round 1, they excluded private equity groups from the process altogether due to that segment's need to use significant amounts of debt and to resell the business several years later. In Round 2, they picked buyers to meet with based on initial indications of interest. Round 3 focused on really getting to know each of the three finalists, determining that two were ultimately poor strategic fits. This left Grayhill as the lone finalist in Round 4.

Remember this framework as you and your M&A advisor work through your sale process. There is more to a deal than price.

## CLEARLY UNDERSTAND YOUR POST-CLOSING ROLE

A final note on creating success by focusing on more than price alone. During the in-depth dating phase of Round 3, make sure to have a candid and clear discussion with each buyer about your ideal role with the business going forward. Do you want to step away from the business as quickly as possible to retire or move on to a new, unrelated venture? Do you want to continue actively running the business and lead it on to new heights? Regardless of what your ideal involvement scenario looks like, understanding how each buyer reacts to your desired role and coming to clear agreement on the length, scope, and compensation of your post-closing involvement is vital to ensuring a successful M&A outcome.

Remember New Castle, the metal stamping company that sold to Advanced Engineering in Chapter 3? The second factor that contributed to New Castle's successful sale was that its owners took the time to get to know the leadership team at Advanced Engineering before closing the transaction and established a clear set of expectations for the sellers' involvement in the business post-closing.

Unless you are an absentee owner who is completely disconnected from your business, all buyers will want you to stay involved in the company in some capacity for at least a twelve- to eighteen-month transition period. This is designed to ensure that the business shifts smoothly into its next phase of ownership without losing valuable customer, vendor, or employee relationships. At its essence, buyers want to make sure the sellers deliver, and they as acquirers receive, the full value of the business.

Many business owners fall into two camps regarding their involvement post-closing. On the one hand, many nod along, but don't fully understand or internalize what the buyers expect of them post-closing, assuming that it will all work out just fine and that they'll happily do whatever is asked of them once they have millions of dollars in their bank account.

These sellers are in for a rude awakening when, after closing, they are now accountable to the new buyer. They no longer have carte blanche to make the decisions they used to take for granted, and they now must answer to a higher authority when things don't go according to plan. Many business owners who were not actively involved in defining their post-closing role with the buyer prior to consummating the deal choose to leave their companies prematurely, jeopardizing the success of the transaction and often leaving deferred compensation on the table.

On the other hand, some business owners are paralyzed into never selling their business by the fear of losing their independence and becoming part of a larger reporting structure. Many entrepreneurs have left jobs in corporate America, or never took them in the first place, because of their desire to control their own destiny. It is this drive that leads to new businesses being formed every day around the world. So, how can they be comfortable with the idea that they'll now have a "boss"?

Business owners in both camps should heed the same advice. First, take the time to really get to know your potential acquirers to determine where the highest level of trust lies, and then fully engage in meaningful planning with the selected buyer about the duration and expanse of your role post-closing. By taking this step seriously as part of their sale process, New Castle's owners knew exactly what they were signing up for in their four-year transition plan with Advanced Engineering. Bolstered by their team of next-generation leaders who would step up as the owners stepped back, New Castle's owners were fully on-board with the reporting structure and operational responsibilities and constraints that existed under Advanced Engineering's ownership. As a result, the transaction was a clear success for both the sellers and the buyer.

* * *

Broaden your focus beyond price when selling your business. Consider such intangible factors such as culture, shared strategic visions, and the role you will be expected to play post-closing. Other influencers include the buyer's reputation in the market, its financial health and recent performance, its ownership composition, and the capital structure of the company post-closing. All these factors will contribute to the overall success or failure of an M&A transaction.

In the next chapter, we'll learn how important it is to eliminate surprises during the M&A process, particularly in the final Phase III portion where they can be most damaging.

## ACTION ITEMS
- *Use the Four-Step Process.* Take to heart the selection process described in this chapter as you approach the subject of which buyers to contact and which suitor you

ultimately select. By alternating between qualitative and quantitative factors, you will not waste time with buyers who aren't good fits and focus your energy on maximizing the outcome of your sale process with those buyers that are ideally suited to carry your business forward.

- *Have a candid conversation about post-closing roles.* As the field of buyers narrows, make sure to have a forthright and direct discussion with each suitor around your ideal role with the business after the transaction closes. Include specifics like full- or part-time, minimum and maximum duration, decision-making authority, and of course, compensation and other executive benefits. Listen carefully to how buyers respond and do your best to visualize yourself working for each buyer under the described circumstances. If something about the top bidder's post-closing plans for you doesn't sit well with you, it is worth stepping back and reconsidering if that buyer really is the best choice.

# CHAPTER 10

# MINIMIZE SURPRISES

———

*"Were you aware that Rick, Winterfield Supply's CEO, is a convicted felon?"*

This was not the question I wanted to hear from Winterfield's buyer ten days before closing. An old adage in the world of mergers and acquisitions is both simple and true: *time kills all deals.* The more time that passes when selling a business, the more likely something will come up to throw things off track. While the passage of time gets the blame in this pearl of wisdom, the real deal-killing culprit is *surprises.*

This was a particularly difficult surprise.

M&A deals fail to close for many reasons. Macro factors, like changes in tax laws, an economic slowdown, or an unexpected rise in interest rates, can cause a transaction to fall apart. Likewise, a sharp decline in the buyer's stock price, a change in strategic direction from their Board of Directors, a shortfall in their bank financing, or some other shift in the buyer's world may lead to them walking away from a deal. In my over twenty years of leading M&A transactions, however, I've seen fully three-quarters of failed M&A deals happen because of an unexpected *seller-related* development, revelation, or discovery. Something comes to light about the target company that the buyer wasn't expecting. To a buyer evaluating an acquisition, surprises from the seller mean uncertainty, and uncertainty means risk. In the deal-making world, an increase in the perceived risk of a transaction without something to offset it, usually a purchase price reduction, upsets the risk/reward balance in the buyer's mind. They may still like the business and want to buy it, but they will pay less for a business that has more risk.

> In the deal-making world, an increase in the perceived risk of a transaction without something to offset it, usually a purchase price reduction, upsets the risk/reward balance in the buyer's mind. They may still like the business and want to buy it, but they will pay less for a business that has more risk.

On the other hand, sellers don't typically believe that the surprising event warrants lowering the purchase price because, from their perspective, the value of the business itself hasn't changed. Being closer to the business than the buyer, sellers aren't alarmed by surprises in their own company as easily. They see it as part of the normal course of business, its regular ups and downs.

Therein lies the root of most failed M&A deals. When a negative surprise leads a buyer to believe a business is riskier than they had thought and the sellers offer no offsetting concessions, buyers will often walk away from a deal.

## HEIGHTENED SENSITIVITY DURING THE FINAL PHASE OF THE PROCESS

While negative surprises can impact an M&A transaction at any time during the process, the period between signing a Letter of Intent (LOI) with a potential buyer and closing that deal is especially sensitive for two main reasons.

1. During this period, sellers agree to provide exclusivity to the buyer for a period of forty-five to sixty days or more while the buyer conducts due diligence. This means that the sellers can't talk to any competing potential acquirers until either exclusivity expires because the buyer took too long to close or the buyer backs away from the deal. So, sellers lose some negotiating leverage as they cannot solicit competing offers from other interested parties during this phase of the process.

2. Purchase price negotiations during the final phase of the M&A process are a one-way affair. The purchase price agreed to in the LOI will never go up if the buyer finds something unexpectedly positive during diligence, but it certainly is at risk of going down if something negative is discovered. For the seller, the period from signing the LOI to closing is all about defense, protecting the agreed-upon deal from a potential re-trade. So, the quicker this period lasts, the better.

Since unexpected negative developments have the power to derail an M&A transaction, we can focus on what kinds of deal-killing surprises sellers should realistically be able to avoid. We know that there are many unforeseen developments that no one expects to see coming, the purely unlucky occurrences that surprise both the seller and buyer alike. But some surprises can be avoided, and the sources of these self-inflicted wounds are worth exploring and identifying to serve as a lighthouse, warning future sellers away from rocky shores.

## PROACTIVELY DISCLOSE ISSUES TO AVOID SURPRISING THE BUYER

I've seen many examples of avoidable surprises in my deal-making career, most of which led to a lower purchase price, and a few that outright killed the deal. One of the most dramatic and memorable examples is the surprising news that the CEO of the business my team was selling was a convicted felon, as revealed by a routine background check that the buyer performed just prior to closing.

In the weeks leading up to closing a transaction, there are usually a number of routine, check-the-box-type diligence steps that buyers will take to cover their bases and make their risk-management department happy. One of these is ordering background checks on the executive management team of the company being acquired. Next to nothing is ever revealed in these exercises, and the uninteresting results are inevitably stashed away in a deal file somewhere, never to be heard of or thought about again.

I assured the buyer that I was as surprised to learn of Rick's criminal past as they were, while also asking myself how Rick could have failed to mention this to me over the past nine months that we'd been working together. "*It says here in this report that Rick served seven years in federal prison in the 1980s for felony larceny,*" the buyer continued. "*That doesn't sound like a person we would want to partner with.*"

Until they received that report, the buyer's opinion of Rick had been overwhelmingly positive. Rick would continue leading the company post-closing under the buyer's ownership, and suddenly, they were losing faith in him.

After collecting myself, I pushed back. "*Rick has paid his debt to society and has put that part of his life behind him. He has created a very successful business career, without so much as a parking ticket in the past thirty years and is still the same dynamic CEO you know him to be. How is this relevant?*"

Though it took some time, the buyer finally admitted that the issue was not the decades-old felony conviction itself. "*We are about to invest $130 million into buying Winterfield Supply in partnership with Rick, and that requires a high level of trust,*" the buyer explained. "*I can't believe that Rick wasn't upfront about this issue earlier in the process or, at the very least, when he consented to the background check. If he didn't voluntarily disclose this to us, what else is he hiding?*"

Some buyers would view a past criminal conviction by a key member of the target's management team as justifiable grounds for walking away from a deal. Others may be less concerned, believing a second chance was warranted. Neither type of buyer, however, appreciates the surprise of uncovering such a fact on their own without warning. The relationship between a potential buyer and the target's management team, which is incredibly important to the deal's ultimate success, starts to form when both sides meet for the first time, and it slowly builds during the months leading up to closing.

> The relationship between a potential buyer and the target's management team, which is incredibly important to the deal's ultimate success, starts to form when both sides meet for the first time, and it slowly builds during the months leading up to closing.

A known but undisclosed issue that comes to light pre-closing will cast doubt on the trust that the buyer has placed in the seller, often killing the transaction. In the case of Winterfield Supply, Rick's credibility with the buyer was irreparably damaged because of his mishandling of the background check, and the buyer soon walked away from the deal.

\* \* \*

I've seen examples of avoidable surprises in other places, though not as dramatic.

## PRO FORMA ADJUSTMENTS

A private equity partner I've known for years recently complained to me about how often the financial information he first receives on a company for sale is later determined to be significantly inaccurate and/or exaggerated. In many cases, once he learns the true financial picture, the business falls below his firm's minimum size thresholds and they can no longer pursue it. He wastes a fair bit of time gearing up on potential deals that seem to fit the firm's targets only to learn upon closer inspection they do not. Sellers should understand that all buyers will conduct an in-depth investigation into their financial statements, typically by engaging a public accounting firm to conduct a Quality of Earnings review.

> Sellers should understand that all buyers will conduct an in-depth investigation into their financial statements, typically by engaging a public accounting firm to conduct a Quality of Earnings review.

These QofE reports delve deeply into the target company's books and records for the past three years and bring to light any irregular items that have artificially increased earnings, such as unsupported or overstated pro forma adjustments, nonrecurring or unusual sources of income, and accounting positions not consistent with generally accepted accounting principles (GAAP). Issues uncovered by the QofE report most often lead to a purchase price reduction.

Private business owners often manage their companies from a financial perspective with the goal of minimizing taxable income, and therefore their tax bill. While there's nothing wrong with this strategy, it is at cross-purposes with what drives value in a sale process; namely to present as high an earnings level as possible to support a larger purchase price.

To account for this difference in accounting strategies, sellers make adjustments to their company's financial statements to exclude one-time or extraordinary costs, which is perfectly acceptable when reasonably performed. But if the seller gets too aggressive with these pro forma adjustments, or wants to receive full credit for a large, one-time order unlikely ever to be seen again, or is not following GAAP in how they report their financials, potential buyers will find out, causing them to lose faith in the financial statements and, by extension, in the management team that produced the financials. At best, the result is a lower purchase price; at worst, a busted deal.

### CUSTOMER RELATIONSHIPS

Similar to the background check issue discussed previously, misrepresenting the strength of a company's customer relationships is another area rich in potential avoidable negative surprises. The quality of a company's customer base is a key driver of value in a sale process, and sellers are understandably eager to brag on this area of the business. The trick is not to overstate how much your customers want to work with you.

Because of the importance of the seller's customer relationships, a portion of the buyer's due diligence process is focused on verifying how strong the company's relationships are, primarily in two ways:

1. Buyers will conduct diligence calls with your top customers before closing. Given the sensitive nature of having a potential buyer contact your customers before acquiring your business, these are typically scheduled at the end of the process, when everything else is settled. Buyers will usually provide a script of the questions they'd like to cover, and while the seller sets up the calls, they don't participate in the calls themselves. If you've overstated your relationship with one of your top customers, it will come to light during this final buyer diligence step.

2. The Purchase & Sale Agreement, the legal document that defines the terms and conditions of an M&A transaction, contains promises, called Representations & Warranties, that you will make about the current condition of your business. These cover many aspects of your business and give the buyer comfort that there are no hidden faults. Included in the Reps & Warranties will be statements you'll make about your customers. For example, you have not been notified by a customer that they will be moving away from you next year. If there were such an instance, you would have to disclose it to the buyer prior to closing.

It is much smarter to be transparent from the beginning with buyers. All companies have customer relationships that could be stronger. Being forthright about the strengths and weaknesses of your account relationships will avoid negative surprises down the road and the distrust that ensues. It will also leave time to create a compromise structure around a problematic customer situation, if one exists. No good comes from a customer issue that is discovered by the buyer at the eleventh hour.

* * *

Unavoidable surprises will always arise without warning to derail a sales process. Life is unpredictable, and a good M&A advisor will help you work through surprises in the best possible way. But business owners would be wise to take steps to eliminate, or at the least minimize, surprises that could have been avoided with preparation and a proactive approach. Eliminating self-inflicted wounds caused by predictable surprises will keep your deal moving forward and significantly improve the likelihood of a successful outcome.

In the final chapter, we'll see how complexity in deal structuring can quickly derail an M&A transaction and why keeping the legal and economic details as simple as possible is most often the best strategy for a successful outcome.

### ACTION ITEMS
- *Be upfront.* If you are preparing to sell your business or are currently amid an M&A process and are aware of potentially damaging information, assume that the issue will come to light at some point before closing. It could be something related to the management team, a wavering customer, or an employee harassment case. Consider how much better the potential buyer would receive it if you disclosed it preemptively, in the appropriate manner, rather than have them discover it on their own. You may

still need to agree on how to handle the issue, but the positive trust created by the former strategy is just as powerful as the negative distrust sewn by the latter.

- *Don't go overboard on financial adjustments.* An experienced M&A advisor will help you present to buyers an appropriately aggressive level of adjusted earnings that will ultimately withstand a buyer's Quality of Earnings review. Using legitimate and justifiable pro forma adjustments is a smart way to drive higher value for your company. Going too far, however, can backfire and lead to the buyer's losing faith in your credibility. For example, owners active in their business will often pay themselves above-market compensation. Adding back the portion of their above-market comp, as well as any other owner-related expenses running through the business that won't continue under new ownership, is entirely appropriate. Excluding from the earnings base *all* the comp received by an owner actively involved in the business, however, is disingenuous, as it doesn't reflect the cost of replacing the role they play post-closing (unless they're willing to work for free).

# CHAPTER 11

# KEEP IT SIMPLE

———

One challenge that sellers often face in the final closing phase of the transaction is the onset of deal fatigue, exhaustion that often turns into hopelessness that the deal will never close, that the process will stretch on endlessly. The danger of deal fatigue is real, as the Browns learned firsthand.

## DEAL COMPLEXITY LEADS TO DEAL FATIGUE

Over the past twenty-five years, Bill and Suzie Brown had worked hard to build a successful security integration business, Chesdin Security, which installed and monitored security systems in commercial, institutional, and residential buildings. The company had reached just over $40 million in annual sales and benefited from a loyal customer base that provided a significant amount of recurring aftermarket repair work, which is more attractive than project-based work.

Now in their early sixties, Bill and Suzie planned to retire over the next five years and considered selling Chesdin Security. *"As planning for retirement became more tangible, we realized that the bulk of our net worth was tied up in the business,"* Bill remembers. *"With no family members or key employees that might want to buy the business, we started focusing on third-party buyers."* They knew that a potential buyer would most likely want them to remain with the business for several years to ensure a smooth transition. And since the business was performing well and they still had several years until retirement, they concluded that now was indeed the right time to start the process, allowing for up to a year to find and close a deal with a buyer and several years thereafter to remain with the business before retiring.

Heeding the advice they received from a friend who had successfully sold his family business, Bill and Suzie interviewed several investment banking firms to represent them in the sale process. *"We were looking for an investment banker who was both highly experienced and also represented a strong fit on a personal level given how important this sale was to us and the amount of time we'd be working together,"* Suzie noted. After comparing notes on what they perceived as the strengths and weaknesses of each of the four investment banks they met, they chose a firm they believed fit both qualifications best. They also engaged a respected regional law firm with a strong business law practice specializing in mergers and acquisitions, ensuring the couple's interests would be well-represented.

The investment banking team gathered the information they needed from the Browns to draft a thorough Confidential Information Memorandum about Chesdin Security. This document covered a wide range of topics, including the company's history, operations, employees, customers, financials, and growth opportunities. Happy with the CIM and list of potential buyers the investment bank created, Bill and Suzie gave their approval for the marketing phase to begin. Given the attractiveness of Chesdin Security's business model, which was less dependent on new construction activity than most security integrators due to their high mix of aftermarket service work, as well as the Browns' willingness to remain active in the business for several years after the deal closed, several buyers expressed interest in the deal.

The Browns met with four of the most aggressive potential buyers in a series of management presentations arranged by their investment bankers, and after reflecting on the meetings, Bill and Suzie agreed on a clear favorite. They picked a small private investment firm, Cooper Lane, eager to acquire Chesdin Security as part of their plan to consolidate the security integration market on a multistate basis. Cooper Lane and the Browns reached an agreement on price, six times the company's earnings of $4 million for a purchase price of $24 million. The Browns signed a Letter of Intent with Cooper Lane, which then engaged its accountants and other third-party advisors to conduct the necessary due diligence to close the transaction. The Browns were excited that their retirement plan was proceeding just as they had planned, though the process was about to take a turn for the worst.

The Browns had agreed in the Letter of Intent (LOI) that 25 percent, or $6 million, of the total purchase price would be structured in the form of an earn-out. Their investment banker told them that earn-outs, which represent deferred purchase price that is only to be paid if the business meets certain agreed-upon performance hurdles after closing, were common in sales of family-run businesses where the sellers were still active. *"While everyone would prefer 100 percent cash at closing, we got comfortable with the structure of $18 million at closing and $6 million in an earn-out,"* Bill recalls. He and Suzie knew they'd continue to lead the business for the next several years and had confidence in their ability to maintain or even accelerate Chesdin's growth, so they were comfortable agreeing to a three-year earn-out in the LOI.

In the Brown's excitement to start the closing process as quickly as possible and move one step closer to retirement, they agreed to fill in the details of the earn-out later as part of negotiating the necessary legal closing documents. Although a common mistake made by many sellers, the Browns did not realize that this decision to put off finalizing an important aspect of the deal would soon come back to haunt them.

After forty-five days of working with Cooper Lane and its advisers to complete financial and business diligence and finding no significant issues, the time came for the final legal negotiations. The primary closing document, the Purchase and Sale Agreement, covers all aspects of the transaction, including the precise details on how the earn-out would be calculated and paid to the Browns over the three years following closing.

The Browns' investment banker proposed a complex structure for the earn-out, which included several features designed to protect the Browns in various scenarios, including a multiyear catch-up provision. This meant that if the business didn't achieve the agreed-upon threshold in year one or year two, but did meet the collective goal for all three years combined, the full amount of the earn-out would still be paid. The buyer and their legal counsel, another high-profile law firm on par with the Browns' attorneys, were receptive to the concept, but this created a whole new set of possibilities under various post-closing scenarios that had to be addressed and negotiated.

Days turned into weeks, and weeks into months, as the attorneys from both sides, together with the Browns and their investment bankers, tried to hash out the fine points of the earn-out construct through hours-long conference calls and dueling drafts of legalese that neither side felt quite captured everything adequately. Bill recalls, *"Here I was, a master electrician and leader of a very successful business, yet with zero training in how to structure M&A transactions. Suzie and I didn't understand half of the things we heard on those negotiating calls, but we were too intimidated to ask."* They understandably started to tune out and trusted that their advisors would take care of it.

Finally, one morning over breakfast, a full four months after the LOI was signed and with no end to the negotiations in sight, Bill turned to Suzie and said, *"I think I've had enough of this process. I'm so lost, I don't even know how much we are selling the company for, much less when we'll actually receive the money."* Suzie agreed; they both realized that deal fatigue had set in, and that they needed to stop the sale process.

*"It was a tough decision; we'd come so far and spent quite a bit of money on advisors up to that point. But the transaction had become too complex,"* Suzie recalls. They called their investment banker later that morning and told them the deal

was off. Buyer Cooper Lane was surprised and disappointed when they heard the news, as were the advisors on both sides. Everyone but the Browns thought the deal was still on track, just taking longer than expected. They all underestimated the level of frustration building with the sellers.

After spending a long weekend at their cabin in the Blue Ridge mountains to get away from work, Bill and Suzie reflected on the failed transaction. They were disappointed and frustrated; they thought they'd done everything right. They'd started the sale process at the right time, well ahead of their targeted retirement date. They'd engaged experienced investment bankers and attorneys to advise them, and they'd carefully chosen their preferred buyer after a well-run process.

In hindsight, though, they realized that they'd fallen victim to an over-reliance on their advisors. First-time sellers should make sure they fully understand the deal that their advisors are negotiating on their behalf, asking questions when necessary, even those that seem naïve or basic. Having selected an M&A advisor with which the Browns had a good rapport, they should have been more comfortable speaking up when they felt like they were falling behind.

Most importantly, sellers should feel empowered to rein in their advisors if the transaction becomes too complex, which can happen among accomplished deal professionals that sometimes equate "more complex" with "thorough." When M&A advisors and attorneys get into a cycle of adding more and more complexity to the structure of a transaction, often in the name of addressing every possible scenario no matter how unlikely, the effect is like the frog in the pot: the heat imperceptibly increases until the water is boiling and the frog and the deal are cooked.

Layer upon layer of complication can build to the point that even experienced advisors miss the fact that they've gone past their clients' comfort zone. Keeping the lines of communication open between advisor and client helps alleviate this issue, but sometimes, a direct dialog across the table is necessary to get a wayward deal back on track. It is common at critical moments in transaction negotiations that the buyers and sellers communicate directly with each other to navigate a potential impasse.

> It is common at critical moments in transaction negotiations that the buyers and sellers communicate directly with each other to navigate a potential impasse.

In nearly every transaction, the buyer and seller can settle all but a few remaining deal issues by working through their attorneys and advisors. Once this point is reached, a "Principal to Principal" telephonic or, preferably, in-person meeting is needed. In nearly every case, the final points are easily agreed upon when the buyer and seller connect directly. Had the Browns sat down with Cooper Lane when they realized the negotiations had started to take on a life of their own, they would likely have been able to work out a simplified handshake deal that the advisors could then have documented. Instead, both sides walked away empty-handed, having wasted valuable time and money on a failed sale process.

* * *

Investment bankers and M&A attorneys play critical roles throughout the M&A process, and I strongly recommend all sellers engage both types of advisors. They bring years of hands-on, closed deal experience to the table to advise their clients, many of whom are going through the M&A sale process for the first time. A common fault of many advisors, though, is a tendency to overcomplicate an issue or deal point in the name of robustly advocating for their client. Ultimately, the buyer and seller are the decision-makers, not the advisors. They must agree on the final deal and sign on the dotted line.

To ensure the best chance for success, buyer and seller should keep a direct line of communication open between them for use at critical junctures, and they should default to the simplest available solution to resolve outstanding issues as often as possible. These will help ensure that deal fatigue doesn't set in and crater an otherwise successful exit transaction on the verge of closing.

## ACTION ITEMS

- *Capture major economic points in the LOI.* As much as possible, come to an agreement with the buyer on the primary economic deal points in the LOI, prior to spending significant time in the due diligence phase of the process. Not only do sellers have more negotiating leverage prior to executing the LOI, but this strategy also ensures that everyone is clear about the financial structure and there will be no surprises later on down the line.

- **Aim for simplicity.** For most sellers, simpler is better. Avoid complex deal structures, whether suggested by your advisors or proposed by the buyer. They will cost you more in legal fees to negotiate and document than a more basic deal. More importantly, a simple structure will ensure both sides clearly understand how the economics of the transaction will work, which isn't always the case when highly complex structures are involved.

- **Maintain a Principal-to-Principal line of communication.** Easily 75 percent of the transaction communication during the final Closing phase of an M&A transaction occurs between each side's M&A and legal advisors. They are the professionals whose mission is to represent their client's interests in facilitating the best deal possible. That said, ultimately the deal is an agreement directly between the buyer and the seller. Whether the seller will exit or remain with the business post-closing, it is important that the principals for both sides trust each other and understand each other's perspectives on deal sticking points. Having the ability to present why a deal point is important to you directly to the buyer, and hearing their perspective in return, will most often lead to a compromised position that both sides can agree to.

- **Beware of deal fatigue.** As we've learned in this book, successfully selling your business involves a lengthy, time-intensive M&A process that can be emotionally charged and pressure-filled. You've got a lot riding on it, and you don't want to mess it up. Once you have an LOI in place with a buyer, it may feel like you're approaching the finish line, but in reality, a few more stages to the race are still there. Keep your energy up and look out for signs of deal fatigue setting in. Rely on your M&A advisor to manage the diligence process and your attorney to manage the legal negotiations; both professionals should make sure their respective tracks are not dragging on too long. If you do start to feel like the process is never-ending and may not be worth the effort, take a step back to gain perspective. Before calling off a deal, which sometimes may be the right decision, I'd recommend one last direct call or meeting with the buyer to see if there's a way to get things back on track.

# CONCLUSION

———

I am the world's biggest fan of business owners.

The thing I love most about my chosen profession of investment banking is that I can work closely with amazing and inspirational entrepreneurs, business leaders, and executives from a variety of industries and regions of our country and help them achieve their exit goals. For most of my clients, the sale of their company is a life-changing financial event for themselves and their families. They have invested so much of themselves, including their time, expertise, emotion, and capital, into building their business, and my job then is to help them, their companies, and their employees find a successful path to their respective next chapters. My clients place a tremendous amount of trust in me as their M&A advisor, and I take my responsibility to them seriously.

> My clients place a tremendous amount of trust in me as their M&A advisor, and I take my responsibility to them seriously.

With that context, my mission in writing this book was to create a resource for business owners and their trusted advisors that captures insider lessons, which I've learned over the course of my career, that you can leverage to your benefit as you work toward a future exit event. I hope I've accomplished that mission.

Whether you read this book from cover to cover or jumped around to those sections that interested you most, I hope you gained a better understanding of how you can make the most of your future exit process. In this book, I wanted to instill in you the same passion and excitement I have for the art of the M&A exit. I hope you see this book as a tool to help you take actionable steps today that will drive a more successful outcome (however you define "successful") when the time comes for your exit.

If you would like to learn more about how I can help you implement these and other strategies from $100 million exits, reach out to me at *jonathan@brabrandenterprises.com* or *https://www.linkedin.com/in/jbrabrand/*.

To make this book a more useful resource guide, I have captured the recommended action items from each chapter below. You can use this index as a reminder of the high-level themes of a particular topic as the need arises along your exit journey.

## ACTION ITEMS

### CHAPTER 1 — DEVELOP INDUSTRY RELATIONSHIPS

- *Plant seeds for the future.* Think strategically about which types of partners, investors, or buyers will take your company to the next level. Conduct research to pick specific targets and use LinkedIn, industry tradeshows, or cold calling to establish contact. Schedule informal meetings, ideally in person, with each group to share insights and your near-term goals, following up on the status of those on the next visit.

- *Incorporate market intel into your growth strategy.* Make note of the key takeaways and insights from your industry conversations and incorporate relevant pieces into your strategic plan. How valuable would it be to know what a potential buyer in your industry is looking for while there's still time to shape your company in that mold? While you may not implement every bit of intel you receive, make note of them all, use what makes sense for where you want to take your company, and file the rest away to revisit twelve to twenty-four months later.

### CHAPTER 2 — RUN YOUR BUSINESS LIKE A PRO

- *Take a new approach to your role.* As the leader of your business, one of your primary responsibilities is to make sure that your company has a strategic plan that includes the following three critical aspects.

  - First, the plan must incorporate the market landscape and your company's competitive strengths and weaknesses relative to other industry participants. A traditional SWOT (strengths, weaknesses, opportunities, and threats) analysis can help here.

- Second, your plan should acknowledge the various real-world constraints that exist, including those related to financial capital and human capital, and work within them. Also, consider the related costs and benefits of removing one or more of these constraints.

- Third, the plan should ensure the company's resources are being put to their highest and best use. This includes everything from whether your products or services are targeting the most valuable end users, to whether your higher-paid employees could better leverage their time with the addition of lower-paid support resources.

- *Refine, implement, and revisit your plan.* Once you have developed your strategic plan, track specific data to measure your performance against plan, and then report your results to an outside accountability partner. Manage your business as if you already have a formal Board of Directors or an outside ownership group that will hold you accountable for delivering performance against your annual plan. Revisit your plan on a quarterly or annual basis and archive historical plans for future reference.

### CHAPTER 3 — BUILD A BUSINESS, NOT A JOB

- *Build your bench.* Look around your organization and identify key individuals that could grow into long-term leaders for your business. Each of your top positions, including your role as President or CEO, should have an identified understudy. If holes exist, make it a priority to fill these positions. Invest in providing training and professional development for those individuals. Consider creating a long-term incentive program to retain them and allow them to participate in the value creation of the business over time. Talk with your attorney and accountants about programs such as options, phantom stock, and profit interests to accomplish this objective.

- *Slowly back away.* Start delegating responsibilities as soon as possible. If necessary, begin slowly with small tasks or for short periods of time, such as while you're away on vacation. Provide mentoring, clear feedback, and support, with the goal of developing managers who can step into your shoes in the future. Remember, having your succession plan in place, even though it isn't yet complete, is significantly better than not having started one at all.

### CHAPTER 4 — KNOW WHEN THE TIME IS RIGHT

- *Look outward.* Look into the current health of the M&A market to see how active it is. An M&A advisor can offer free insights into M&A activity overall and within your industry sector (we'll learn more about them in the next chapter). Assess the health of your industry and grade its outlook. Are you seeing consolidation or other M&A activity within your industry and among your competitors? If so, it may indicate that the external conditions are optimal for a sale.

- **Look inward.** Take a step back and strategically evaluate where your business is in its corporate evolution and whether you have the energy and expertise needed to lead it forward. Is the company reaching an inflection point where new ownership could shift the business into a higher gear? Are some opportunities not pursued for lack of capital, expertise, or talent? Consider what new chapters a sale would bring for you, for the company, and for your employees.

### CHAPTER 5 — ENGAGE AN M&A ADVISOR

- **Engage an expert.** When you sell your company, use an M&A advisor; they more than pay for themselves and yield significantly better results than going it alone. Next, only consider firms that focus on your company's transaction size and have an impeccable reputation, as they will be representing your company to the market. Then make your final selection based on spending time with the specific professionals who will be staffed on your deal and ask questions of them. Do they have experience with similar transactions? Do they have available capacity and aren't spread too thin on too many simultaneous projects? Will senior team members be active throughout the process or disappear after landing you as a client and hand you off to junior staff? Most importantly, do you trust the people on the team?

- *Fight the urge to rush.* Though some or all of the excuses in this chapter may come to you, resist them. Make up your mind to be proactive, to be well-prepared, to be ahead of the game when you complete Phase I and start contacting buyers. Critically analyze your business from a hypothetical buyer's perspective and think about what data you would like to review to really understand what is happening with your company. What areas of the business model may seem weak or risky to an outside party at first glance? What metrics do you track that give you comfort in those areas? Having a repository of analyses handy to provide to buyers proactively or immediately upon request will increase your professional credibility and keep the process momentum high.

- *Take an appropriately aggressive approach to EBITDA adjustments.* Avoid the temptation to overdo it regarding making adjustments to your company's EBITDA. A desire to maximize the purchase price must be balanced against maintaining credibility and goodwill with the buyer, who at some point before closing will go through every EBITDA adjustment in excruciating detail and will make their own determination about which are acceptable versus too aggressive. Appendix A provides a sample list of acceptable EBITDA adjustments you can use to guide your thinking here. Make sure you have supporting documentation for each one ready for buyer confirmation later.

- *Think creatively and expansively about your company.* Rather than describe exactly what your company does today at ground level, pull back and view it from cruising altitude. Think about what value you provide to customers and what related types of products or services they also value. Think too about what new types of customers might also value your current offering. Then try to capture all of that in your positioning. Not only will it help drive increased value for your business with the most likely buyers, but it will also increase the likelihood that your company will attract more tangential buyers and add competitive pressure to your M&A process.

## CHAPTER 8 — UNDERSTAND YOUR OPTIONS

- *Start with an open mind.* As you think about a future buyer for your business, take a fresh perspective and consider a wide variety of buyers, including strategic and financial buyers. Consider not only direct competitors, but also tangential strategic buyers that may view your company as complementary or as a means to enter new markets or customer segments.

- *Consider your appetite for continued leadership.* Are you viewing an exit as a well-deserved means to fully retire and enjoy the financial rewards from having successfully built a business? Or would you like to continue to lead the business through its next phase of growth, but with additional capital for growth or personal net worth diversification? If you are planning to transition out of the business in the near term, are there successors in place that can step into your leadership shoes? No right or wrong answers exist for these and other related questions, but listen to your responses and let them shape which types of buyers to contact during your sale process.

### CHAPTER 9 — FOCUS ON MORE THAN PRICE

- *Use the Four-Step Process.* Take to heart the selection process described in this chapter as you approach the subject of which buyers to contact and which suitor you ultimately select. By alternating between qualitative and quantitative factors, you will not waste time with buyers who aren't good fits and focus your energy on maximizing the outcome of your sale process with those buyers that are ideally suited to carry your business forward.

- *Have a candid conversation about post-closing roles.* As the field of buyers narrows, make sure to have a forthright and direct discussion with each suitor around your ideal role with the business after the transaction closes. Include specifics like full- or part-time, minimum and maximum duration, decision-making authority, and of course, compensation and other executive benefits. Listen carefully to how buyers respond and do your best to visualize yourself working for each buyer under the described circumstances. If something about the top bidder's post-closing plans for you doesn't sit well with you, it is worth stepping back and reconsidering if that buyer really is the best choice.

- *Be upfront.* If you are preparing to sell your business or are currently amid an M&A process and are aware of potentially damaging information, assume that the issue will come to light before closing. It could be related to the management team, a wavering customer, or an employee harassment case. Consider how much better the potential buyer would receive it if you disclosed it preemptively, in the appropriate manner, rather than have them discover it on their own. You may still need to agree on how to handle the issue, but the positive trust created by the former strategy is just as powerful as the negative distrust sown by the latter.

- *Don't go overboard on financial adjustments.* An experienced M&A advisor will help you present to buyers an appropriately aggressive level of adjusted earnings that will ultimately withstand a buyer's Quality of Earnings review. Using legitimate and justifiable pro forma adjustments is a smart way to drive higher value for your company. Going too far, however, can backfire and lead to the buyer's losing faith in your credibility. For example, owners active in their business will often pay themselves above-market compensation. Adding back the portion of their above-market comp, as well as any other owner-related expenses running through the business that won't continue under new ownership, is entirely appropriate. Excluding from the earnings base *all* the comp received by an owner actively involved in the business, however, is disingenuous, as it doesn't reflect the cost of replacing the role they play post-closing (unless they're willing to work for free).

- *Capture major economic points in the LOI.* As much as possible, come to an agreement with the buyer on the primary economic deal points in the LOI, prior to spending significant time in the due diligence phase of the process. Not only do sellers have more negotiating leverage prior to executing the LOI, but this strategy also ensures that everyone is clear about the financial structure and there will be no surprises later on down the line.

- *Aim for simplicity.* For most sellers, simpler is better. Avoid complex deal structures, whether suggested by your advisors or proposed by the buyer. They will cost you more in legal fees to negotiate and document than a more basic deal. More importantly, a simple structure will ensure both sides clearly understand how the economics of the transaction will work, which isn't always the case when highly complex structures are involved.

- *Maintain a Principal-to-Principal line of communication.* Easily 75 percent of the transaction communication during the final Closing phase of an M&A transaction occurs between each side's M&A and legal advisors. They are the professionals whose mission is to represent their client's interests in facilitating the best deal possible. That said, ultimately the deal is an agreement directly between the buyer and the seller. Whether the seller will exit or remain with the business post-closing, it is important that the principals for both sides trust each other and understand each other's perspectives on deal sticking points. Having the ability to present why a deal point is important to you directly to the buyer, and hearing their perspective in return, will most often lead to a compromised position that both sides can agree to.

- **Beware of deal fatigue.** As we've learned in this book, successfully selling your business involves a lengthy, time-intensive M&A process that can be emotionally charged and pressure filled. You've got a lot riding on it, and you don't want to mess it up. Once you have an LOI in place with a buyer, it may feel like you're approaching the finish line, but in reality, a few more stages to the race are still there. Keep your energy up, and look out for signs of deal fatigue setting in. Rely on your M&A advisor to manage the diligence process and your attorney to manage the legal negotiations; both professionals should make sure their respective tracks are not dragging on too long. If you do start to feel like the process is never-ending and may not be worth the effort, take a step back to gain perspective. Before calling off a deal, which sometimes may be the right decision, I'd recommend one last direct call or meeting with the buyer to see if there's a way to get things back on track.

# ACKNOWLEDGMENTS

———

First and foremost, I'd like to thank my amazing wife, Danessa, who encouraged me to start the journey to publish a book and inspired me every step of the way. She is my trusted partner in this endeavor and in all aspects of my life. Thank you; I would never have accomplished this without you.

Thank you to all my interviewees. Thank you for taking time out of your busy schedules to share your stories of M&A successes and failures with me. They bring a richness to this book that would otherwise have been dull and academic. Given the confidential nature of our conversations, I am unable to give you credit here by name, but you know who you are. Thank you.

Thank you to my executive coach, Jay Fehnel, who helped me become a better version of myself, for introducing me to the Creators Institute.

Thank you to Eric Koester, who has an amazing gift for creating first-time authors, and for the team at New Degree Press, especially Brian Bies and my editors, Alexander Pyles and Heather Gomez.

And thank you to everyone who preordered copies of this book to make publishing possible, spread the word about *The $100 Million Exit* to gather amazing momentum, and helped me publish a book I am proud of. I am sincerely grateful for all your support.

Danessa Knaupp*
Eric Koester
DanaDee & Jim Carragher
Lou Marmo
Tim Stapleton
Jay Fehnel*
Kyle & Pete Laver
Bianca & Chris Bryan
Ian Batt
Matthew Riffe
Todd Mawyer*
Beau & Tiffany Waldrop
Erin Watkins Quinn
David & Jenny Sharrar*
Kelley Powell

Nancy Eberhardt
Stan Maupin
Sean Kelley
Schon Williams
Dan Rodenhaver
Jay Bloxsom
Andy & Betty Brabrand*
Keith Middleton*
Rich Reinecke*
Brian Sykora
Scot McRoberts
Bram Hall
Ben English
Jeff Hammer

* A very special thanks to these supporters who preordered multiple copies.

# APPENDIX A

# REPRESENTATIVE EBITDA ADJUSTMENTS

––––

Below is a sample list of nonrecurring, shareholder-related, or extraordinary items that should be excluded from the presentation of your company's financial statements during a sale process. While this list is not meant to be exhaustive or comprehensive, it should convey a sense of the types of income and expense items that can be adjusted out of the financial results that you present to potential buyers to present your company's normalized earnings-generating capacity. Remember to build a repository of supporting documentation and calculations to support each of your proposed addbacks, as buyers will want to verify them in detail during their due diligence prior to closing.

Excessive (above-market) compensation or perks to owners, management, and employees
Personal legal costs for estate planning, divorce, personal litigation, etc.

Tuition and educational expenses for children and family members

Monetary donations to charitable organizations

Golf, country club, or other lifestyle expenses not necessary to the business

Nepotism expenses (salary, autos, computers, vacations, etc.)

Vacations or other related-party travel expenses, including time-share expenses, etc.

Multiple vehicles or unusual vehicle expenses for the owner, family, etc.

Excessive insurance to owners and related parties (e.g., life, health, disability)

Building rent paid to an owner in excess of (or under) market rates

Equipment leases paid to an owner in excess of (or under) market rates

Professional sports tickets not necessary for the business

Rental expenses or repairs that would normally be paid by an unrelated landlord

Hobbies such as buying jewelry, antique cars, etc.

Below-market transfers of assets to related parties or family members

Costs paid in excess of market to vendors that are related parties or friends

Discounts or free delivery given to related parties or friends

Repairs, remodeling, maintenance, insurance, or other expenses for a personal residence

Inventory or scrap sold for cash and not deposited into the company's bank account

Alimony or child-support payments made by the company

Maintenance, IT, or other costs that were expensed but could be capitalized

Write-off of an unproductive or obsolete asset

Unusual, one-time or prior-period adjustments proposed by independent CPAs

Legal expenses incurred for the exit strategy

Legal costs of restructuring or reorganization

Audit, appraisal, or consulting fees for the exit strategy

Costs of engaging an M&A advisor

Litigation expenses that have concluded and are nonrecurring

Costs of exits of minority owners prior to the sale of the company

Insurance claims

One-time costs associated with opening a new facility

Inventory write-off that is unusual or nonrecurring

Unusual bad-debt expenses, such as a chapter 11 bankruptcy filing by a customer

Executive employment costs, such as signing bonus, relocation package, severance, or other nonrecurring expenses

Large and unusual bonuses or other compensation paid for nonrecurring transactions

Professional fees, such as creating a Defined Contribution or Benefit Plan

Leases that were expensed instead of being capitalized

Equipment that was expensed instead of being capitalized

One-time marketing, branding, public relations, or research costs

# APPENDIX B

# CITATIONS

———

Capital One Financial Corporation. 1996. "Capturing the Essence of Capital One." Annual Report.

Cerulli Associates. n.d. *The Great Wealth Transfer.* Accessed January 26, 2020. *https://info.cerulli.com/HNW-Transfer-of-Wealth-Cerulli.html.*

GF Data Resources LLC. 2019. "GF Data Highlights and Products 2019." *http://www.gfdata.com*

IBISWorld. 2019. *Used Car Dealers Industry in the US—Market Research Report.* July. Accessed January 26, 2020. *https://www.ibisworld.com/united-states/market-research-reports/used-car-dealers-industry/.*

Musil, Steven. 2008. "FCC approves Sirius-XM satellite radio merger." *CNET,* July 26.

PitchBook Data, Inc. 2019. "3Q 2019 North American M&A Report." Accompanying Worksheet.

PitchBook Data, Inc. 2019. "3Q 2019 US PE Breakdown." Accompanying Worksheet.

Sidley. 2019. "FTC Revises HSR Premerger Notification and Clayton Act § 8 Thresholds and Maximum Per Diem HSR Penalty." Antitrust Update.

Simons, Joseph J., and Makan Delrahim. 2018. "Hart-Scott-Rodino Annual Report: Fiscal Year 2018."

2015. "Statement of FTC Bureau of Competition Director Debbie Feinstein on Sysco and U.S. Foods' Abandonment of Their Proposed Merger." *Federal Trade Commission Press Release. June 29.*

Made in USA - Kendallville, IN
1119209_9781641375177
06.03.2020 0812